WHY CHILDREN NEED JOY

WHY CHILDREN NEED JOY

BEN KINGSTON-HUGHES

S Sage

1 Oliver's Yard
55 City Road
London EC1Y 1SP

2455 Teller Road
Thousand Oaks
California 91320

Unit No 323-333, Third Floor, F-Block
International Trade Tower, Nehru Place
New Delhi 110 019

8 Marina View Suite 43-053
Asia Square Tower 1
Singapore 018960

Editor: Delayna Spencer
Editorial assistant: Harry Dixon
Production editor: Sarah Sewell
Copyeditor: Thea Watson
Proofreader: Bryan Campbell
Cover design: Hayley Davis
Typeset by: C&M Digitals (P) Ltd, Chennai, India
Printed in the UK

Library of Congress Control Number: 2023937123

British Library Cataloguing in Publication data

A catalogue record for this book is available from the British Library

ISBN 978-1-5296-0979-0
ISBN 978-1-5296-0978-3 (pbk)

At Sage we take sustainability seriously. Most of our products are printed in the UK using responsibly sourced papers and boards. When we print overseas we ensure sustainable papers are used as measured by the Paper Chain Project grading system. We undertake an annual audit to monitor our sustainability.

DEDICATION

To Felix and River – my constant sources of joy.

CONTENTS

ABOUT THE AUTHOR

Ben Kingston-Hughes is an author, national award-winning trainer and Managing Director of Inspired Children. He has worked with children for over thirty years and has twice appeared on television working with vulnerable children. His transformative training has been mentioned by Ofsted as an example of outstanding staff development and his distinctive blend of humour, neuroscience and real-life practical experiences make his training invaluable for anyone working with children. He has written articles for several publications including Nursery World magazine. His finest moment was when a group of reception children named their class frog after him.

CHAPTER SUMMARIES

Introduction

Why we absolutely need a book about joy at this time.

1. Simple moments of joy – Why joy is so undervalued and yet so important

This chapter examines exactly what joy is and why it is absolutely vital to the development and well-being of our children. Unpicking the fundamental steps in any aspect of development we see that an essential step is almost completely ignored throughout child development theory. The chapter also looks at joy as a universal concept breaking down barriers of culture, race, gender, age and even language.

2. The joy of goo and big red buses!

The fundamental joy of exploration and sensory feedback. A deep dive into curiosity and the unique biochemistry of sensory play, and how the adult world can take away joy without ever realising it.

3. Expressions of joy – The joy of words and sounds

This chapter unpicks communication and language and shows how joy is a key motivator and integral part of the development process. A look at how humans developed language 200,000 years ago gives us a unique insight into the role of joy and how, far from being an optional extra, it is an essential process. This chapter looks at how joy can support EAL and how singing can change the world (no – quite literally!).

4. The joy of movement and dancing elephants

70 per cent of children currently disengage in sport. Why? Because adults take away the fundamental joy of movement by making it all about winning or achieving. Joy underpins every aspect of early physical development and floods the brain with addictive biochemicals that make you want to move more. This whole process is undermined if the joy is removed. This chapter looks at breaking cycles of inactivity through the application of joy.

5. The joy of poo and a school for ninjas

How early humour is expressed in children, why this is vital and why we should accept the sometimes limited nature of our children's 'jokes'. A look at 'mischief' and how joyful mischievous experiences can actually promote pro-social behaviour.

6. Seek and destroy – The robot teachers are coming!

Yes, we now have robot teachers being trialled in China and Japan. Have these people never watched a *Terminator* film? This chapter looks at what robot teachers can actually do and what they can never ever do. We look at the neuroscience of learning and why a robot teacher may know more facts than a human teacher but can never inspire joy and passion in a subject.

7. Who stole our joy?

This chapter looks at the catastrophic effect of a lack of joy. The chapter looks at the biochemistry of anxiety and how this affects how children play, behave and even learn. We look at teasing and banter and how even well-meaning adults can completely eradicate joy from our children's lives. We also look at the casual bullying that many adults do to children without ever realising, and how many children's experiences of adults are far from positive.

8. We are celestial – Being a different sort of grown-up

Seeing through behaviour to the child underneath. Recognising that negative experiences will impact on a child's behaviour making them neurologically pre-disposed towards less social behaviour. Understanding that most adults in the child's world will also respond negatively. Through joy we can be a different sort of grown-up and profoundly impact on a child.

9. Simple equations for thriving – How compassion and joy can change not just children but our entire society

This final chapter looks at what could happen if we get this right. There are no more excuses to hide behind. The evidence is both compelling and substantial that people who work with children are potentially the most important resource in the world. With joy as our guiding principle we can transform nurseries, schools, afterschool provision and even homes to be an oasis of joy, play and nurturing, to profoundly impact in the future of our children and the world they will inherit. A compelling argument is put forth that joy should be included as the fourth Characteristic of Effective Learning.

INTRODUCTION

What is this book all about?

OK, so this is a book about joy – no don't stop reading yet. I realise that on the surface joy may seem like an abstract concept, but I believe it is one of the most undervalued and underexplored aspects of working with children. Now I know what you are thinking: is Ben having a midlife crisis rambling on about joy? Has he turned into an aging hippy and is he going to tell us all to hug a tree? Well maybe yes to both. The thing is, I think we are missing something here. There is something indefinable that I see almost every time I work with children. Simple moments of joy that have the most profound and transformative effect on our most vulnerable children.

Working with children for over 32 years (what's that? You don't look old enough?) I have seen the profound and life changing difference that simple moments of joy can make to our most vulnerable children. Far too often for it to be a coincidence, I have seen children's lives utterly changed because compassionate adults have given them back something fundamental that they have lost. I believe that a joyful childhood is not just every child's right but an essential process, underpinning every aspect of emotional well-being and development. I believe that joy is a vital life experience and something that all children categorically deserve and need in order to thrive.

I also believe that it is declining. In the light of the pandemic and changes in the life experiences of our children I believe that levels of joy are critically low for many of our children with potentially catastrophic effects on their well-being. I currently work with vulnerable children. Children who have overwhelmingly negative experiences of life but without the balancing moments of joy. To say those children are struggling is an understatement.

So, what is this indefinable concept of joy that seems to have such a profound effect on our children? Joy is a concept that can be the fundamental difference between a child struggling and a child thriving, and yet it is not mentioned in the Early Years Foundation Stage (EYFS) or in the National Curriculum, is absent from the Characteristics of Effective Learning and is rarely mentioned in child development theory. It seems to me that joy is a forgotten concept, especially in light of a global pandemic, and I mean to do something about that. So that is what this book is all about. I am going to define the indefinable and show just how important the concept of joy is for all of our children (and adults too). I am going to put joy on the map, not as an abstract concept but as a concrete, neurologically rich developmental process that is a vital part of every childhood.

On neurotypes

I have ADHD and I really want this book to be accessible to a broad range of neurotypes. I believe our current definitions of 'neurotypical' and 'neuro-diverse' fail to cater for a large number of children and we need to radically re-imagine childhood to support all of our children to thrive. I have written this book in a style that would keep me interested despite my wandering mind, so it does not read like a textbook. I want people to want to read this regardless of whether they are studying early childhood development or simply interested in how we can improve outcomes for children.

On clowns

In my previous book (Kingston-Hughes, 2021) I was a little mean to magicians as they represent a way of working with children that is more about the adult than the child. In this book I may have occasionally been insulting to clowns as they represent an adult version of 'fun' that does not necessarily align with a child's definition. As always, I do not want to cause offence and I know there are some amazing clowns out there (you know who you are Paul!).

On privilege

I have spoken in this book about my own childhood and some of the challenges I faced. Working with a broad range of children with vastly differing social and cultural backgrounds, I cannot stress enough how much of an advantage my own social background has given me. As a white male I have had a very differ-ent experience of society than some of the children and families I work with. I could not write a book about joy without acknowledging the societal bias that effects thousands of children due to race, social background, culture and gender. There may be some people who say this invalidates my position to write about such inequalities and I fully understand that view. I accept that social privilege has given me opportunities not available to others, even to the extent of writing this book. I do still believe I have something valid to say. Having worked for over thirty years with vulnerable children, I believe I have insights into how we can support all of our children to have a better childhood and I hope that readers will understand my genuine passion for a reimagined childhood full of joy for all of our children.

On neuroscience

I am not a neuroscientist. However, I love exploring neuroscience because it gives us a new way to understand our children. I have also found that our society does not always value mental health and emotional well-being as much as it should. Some people switch off when you talk about mental health, but they sit up and listen when you talk about physical changes to the brain. So, I have explored lots of neuroscience themes in this book but only the stuff that directly applies to children. I don't pretend to understand the human brain (I don't believe even neuroscientists fully do!), but I have tried to present the neuroscience theories that back up what I can see in the children I work with. If my explanations are overly simplistic, I hope you will forgive me and do your own research because the human brain is unique, amazing and fascinating.

On names

I switch off when I read about child X interacting with child Y so I have included names in the studies and case studies. Some of these are the real names, where I have permission, but others have been changed. The stories are all real.

Pictures

I can't be bothered to mess about with stock images and clip art, so I have asked children to draw the illustrations for this book. I think this is much better! After all it is a book about children.

So, whether you work with children, have children or ever were a child, sit back, grab some cake and prepare to explore the undervalued, underrepresented and unsung concept of joy.

1
SIMPLE MOMENTS OF JOY — WHY JOY IS SO UNDERVALUED AND YET SO IMPORTANT

A magic potion for joy

I work on adoption activity days, a wonderful project to help children find forever families (a note: the following story is about a child from an ethnic minority, and it is currently statistically harder to find forever families for children from ethnic minorities).

Last year we made magic potions with a group of children and adopters. Our potions are simply made of food colouring and shiny confetti but then we make the potion light up by having a torch cunningly concealed in a cardboard box. A young child had, with the help of an adopter, made a bright green potion. Unaware that the potion was about to light up, the child placed it on top of the light box and then something happened as he saw his potion glow with 'real' magic. The child's eyes widened, and he began shaking. Something appeared to 'bubble' up inside him and then he laughed and, almost as an involuntary reflex, squeezed the potion as hard as he could. Yes, you've guessed it. The lid flew off and the potion exploded out of the bottle hitting the adopter (who was wearing a white shirt) in the face and dousing him in green liquid. There was a moment of silence and then both adopter and child laughed out loud.

What do we mean by joy?

So, what was it this child was experiencing? A feeling so real and visceral that he simply could not stop himself from physically reacting. What actually is joy?

Sometimes joy comes from simple awe and wonder in the world. Sometimes it is experienced through physically doing something such as dancing or singing. It can be the surprise of discovery, such as a magic potion lighting up, and it can also be the sense of achievement when we climb a tree or maybe even solve a sum. Maybe the concept of joy is difficult to define because it can cover so many different situations. Maybe we do not always see its value because we don't always notice when it has gone. The concept of joy is linked to play and many of the ways we see children experiencing joy are through play. Joy is broader than play though. It is a feeling that we may experience through play but a feeling that can also occur through a much broader range of experiences. I believe the feeling of joy is when we have gone beyond the ordinary, a state of being that is profoundly important because it is more powerful than our ordinary experiences of life. So, happy children are fantastic but joyful children are living their best life.

Superhero parents

I regularly deliver play training to parents to help embed more play in the home and they often comment on the post-course evaluation that they were not expecting to enjoy the session as much. To demonstrate the concept of joy I have recently started videoing parents in slow motion whilst they are engaged in superhero play, complete with masks and capes made out of old curtains. I then show the video to the parents at the end of the session. More than any amount of taught information, this simple visual experience demonstrates all of the neuroscience and biochemistry of play and presents a tangible picture of joy. There is something almost magical about a group of adults being super-heroes in slow motion. The joy on their faces is much more obvious than it is at normal speed and is both comical and heart-warming at the same time. All I then need to say to finish the session is, 'Look at your faces in the video, **that is what our children need to experience!'**

My work with parents also shows us some of the barriers to joy. Initially parents are embarrassed and even uncomfortable about simply playing. I never force anyone on the sessions to participate but in almost all cases the parents gradually become swept up in the atmosphere of positive play and begin to join in. This reluctance to engage is clearly a barrier to the joy that we experience when we let go of our adult inhibitions and play. In fact one of the simplest ways we can encourage more joy in our children is to play more as adults.

A unique hug

On one of our parent sessions in an inner-city area we played a chasing game. The group was culturally and socially diverse in an area of the UK that historically has high levels of racial tension. During the catching game an older Asian grandma caught a young, white, working-class dad. Their cultural and social backgrounds could not have been more different yet as the grandma caught the man, they hugged, giggled and then split apart to catch other people. I could not help thinking that the moment of joy they had just shared was, for this area, utterly unique. I could not think of a single other instance in this area when two people from such hugely different backgrounds would hug each other let alone giggle together.

So clearly in this case joy transcended not merely our adult reluctance to play but also long entrenched issues of culture, social background, gender and even age, creating something genuinely special. During the same session I took a photo of a group of parents sat in a den they had made out of some old bits of material, some pegs and chairs. The photo was unremarkable except for the genuine joy on every one of the three participants' faces. This was not a 'say cheese' moment of pretend happiness but a genuine moment of shared joy reflected on each face. It was only afterwards that I remembered that one of the three ladies was not actually a parent but was a translator for another parent in the photo. This meant that two of the people in the photo did not speak the same language. Except in this instance they did. They were all speaking a shared language of joy.

Holiday play

If you are fortunate enough to go on a holiday abroad you may sit around a pool, not talking to the German family on one side or the Spanish family on the other. If you glance over to the pool however you may see your children laughing and splashing with the German children and the Spanish children without speaking a single word of the same language. Joy is not merely a positive feeling but a shared experience with the potential to break down barriers.

What is joy?

So, what actually is joy? This is where things get tricky. Clearly joy is connected to ideas such as happiness, pleasure, fun, excitement, and delight. However, it can also encompass fascination, wonder and awe. There is also joy in being at home or with loved ones, feeling emotionally safe or content. Even happiness, which could be said to be an important component of joy, can represent many feelings. Remember not every happy moment is accompanied by huge smiles and belly laughs. In fact, it may not contain smiles at all. The slow-motion superhero videos are always funny to watch but there is a marked difference in parents' expressions as they play. Some have the wide smiles and laughter one would associate with happiness whilst others have completely serious faces as they become fully immersed in their superhero play. This does not mean that the serious faced parents are less happy than the smiley faced ones. It simply means that we express happiness in different ways.

A happy sigh

I will never forget a child at an afterschool setting who would walk into the setting, throw his bag into a corner and audibly sigh. It was the moment when, after a taxing day at school, he could begin to relax. The sigh was his way of expressing the feelings of safety and contentment at being somewhere he felt valued and important.

A working definition of joy would therefore need to embody all of these threads, one of happiness or contentment (but not necessarily accompanied by smiles and laughter) and another of engagement and stimulation, with an overarching sense of emotional safety. What I believe we are looking at is joy as a fundamental concept combining happiness/contentment and engagement/stimulation in an emotionally secure context that can be felt across a broad range of experiences.

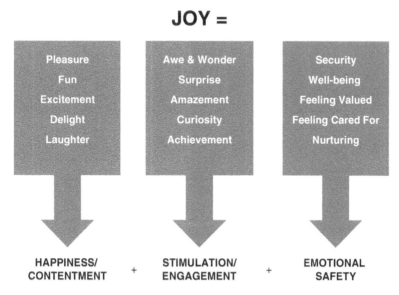

JOY =

Pleasure	Awe & Wonder	Security
Fun	Surprise	Well-being
Excitement	Amazement	Feeling Valued
Delight	Curiosity	Feeling Cared For
Laughter	Achievement	Nurturing

HAPPINESS/ CONTENTMENT + **STIMULATION/ ENGAGEMENT** + **EMOTIONAL SAFETY**

Figure 1.1   Joy equation

OK, so now we are getting somewhere. High levels of happiness with high levels of stimulation whilst feeling safe. Already this seems to tie in with how we know children learn and develop but I think it goes further than that. What I am beginning to describe here is a fundamental formula for thriving children. It is also something really easy to understand and apply to our interactions with children.

Happiness in the brain

As the first part of our equation for joy it would be great if we could see into the brain to see what happens when we experience happiness. You would think, with the latest fMRI (functional magnetic resonance imaging) technology, this should be easy. Simply strap someone into an imaging machine, make them experience joy, flip a switch and see what happens in the brain. If like me, you are imagining Dr Frankenstein cackling madly as lightning flashes, then you probably have a very vivid imagination. Unfortunately, this is not as easy as it might sound. Firstly, the technology is expensive; this means that it is difficult to do a large-scale study. Secondly, how do we make sure we are observing happiness or joy, or in fact any emotion when our brains are constantly active? Lastly, what makes a person happy is completely subjective. You can't just show a group of people a kitten and expect them to experience the same levels of happiness (or horror depending on your view on kittens).

Image 1.1 Frankenstein's monster in a laboratory thinking about kittens by M (I honestly did not think any child would attempt this picture!)

Despite the lack of concrete research into the neuroscience of happiness there are several clues into which bits of the brain may play a role. There are also several biochemicals that are believed to play a significant role in happiness and contentment.

In my previous book about play I talked at length about the biochemicals associated with play. Chemicals such as benzodiazepines, which are a potent anti-anxiety medication, flood the brain when we play (Valium is a benzodiazepine!). When examining the biochemistry of happiness, we also see that biochemicals are hugely significant.

Serotonin

Serotonin is a neurotransmitter that some scientists even refer to as the 'happiness chemical'. Neurotransmitters are our body's chemical messengers carrying messages from one nerve cell across a space to the next nerve cell. Basically, our nerves carry messages around our bodies and are similar to electrical wiring in that they carry electrical impulses around our bodies. Feelings of pain, when we stub our toe for instance, are transmitted to our brain via these nerves. Unlike an electrical system though, our nerve system has gaps in it where the electricity cannot pass. Instead, chemicals are released, called neurotransmitters, that bridge these gaps and carry the messages on to the next nerve cell.

What has this got to do with happiness? Well, it turns out that higher serotonin levels increase feelings of well-being, confidence and belonging. Serotonin appears to be produced in higher amounts when we feel important and valued by those around us. Again, we are starting to see links to a child's experiences. Children who are valued and feel important are more likely to produce serotonin. Children who feel worthless simply don't.

There are several articles online that cite the optimum conditions for children to develop confidence and self-esteem. Almost all of these articles cite 'feeling valued' or 'feeling important' as key criteria for gaining confidence. Now we know that these feelings are not just intrinsically building a child's confidence but are flooding the brain with serotonin. We will come back to how we can help our most vulnerable children feel important later in the book.

Children with lower serotonin levels are much more likely to experience negative feelings and symptoms of depression and people diagnosed with depression are likely to have lower serotonin levels.

I feel it in my stomach

Not all serotonin is produced in the brain and in fact a significant quantity is produced by bacteria in our intestines. That visceral feeling of joy in our stomach could be caused by serotonin, although the current research is far from clear on this.

Dopamine

Dopamine is another neurotransmitter also intrinsically linked to feelings of happiness and contentment. Our body releases dopamine as part of our reward system when we achieve a goal or experience feelings of contentment such as after a delicious meal. It actually plays a part in our efficiency and effectiveness to complete a task and is therefore a key component in learning and development. Children experiencing feelings of success through learning, for instance, will produce dopamine, making them want to learn more to experience more dopamine. Children who feel like they have failed or are constantly told they are wrong will not produce dopamine and consequently may not want to try.

Once again people with lower dopamine levels are much more likely to have symptoms of depression or mood disorders. They are also less able to concentrate and may have difficulty staying on task and remaining focused.

Oxytocin – The nurturing biochemical

When looking for biochemicals associated with happiness then oxytocin may be a contender. It is a neurotransmitter closely linked to nurturing and developing relationships and is produced when we experience social behaviours such as a hug. It is a vital part of parent-child bonding and produced during moments of play together. I spoke briefly about oxytocin in my previous book as it is produced when we play, especially when we play together, and when working with children with insecure attachments it is profoundly important to well-being. Oxytocin is important for long-term happiness and feelings of being loved or cared for, so it is a vital part of the equation for joy that I described earlier.

A unique hug: Part two

I deliver a lot of keynote speeches and so quite often come into contact with motivational speakers. You may have seen these speakers before. They are charismatic, energetic and adept at convincing me I need to be a better person and be nicer to my family. These positive feelings usually last until I actually get home to my family and then it all goes out of the window. One speaker in particular alarmed me when he said, 'If you hug someone you produce oxytocin which makes you feel amazing'. The reason I was alarmed was not because he was incorrect but because at the time, I was sitting at a table with six ladies I had never met before. All I could think was, 'Please don't make me hug someone!' He then made a truly terrifying statement which was, 'If you hug someone for six seconds or longer you increase the amount of positive biochemicals by up to three times. So now I'd like you all to turn to the person next to you and...' At this point I got up and left the room. Now I know that might make me seem antisocial but there was no way I was comfortable hugging a stranger for six agonising seconds. It was particularly awkward because I then had to sneak back in to do my speech.

So, was this motivational speaker wrong or am I just an antisocial monster? Well, maybe he was right and wrong at the same time. He was correct in that a hug is a key method of nurturing and quite definitely produces oxytocin. The problem is that if the person feels awkward or anxious about the hug then they will not be feeling nurtured and will not be producing oxytocin. In all probability they will be producing cortisol, a stress hormone that is genuinely toxic. So, the hug is undeniably a vital form of nurturing but not suitable for every person in every context. In terms of our work with children it is vitally important then, that we tailor our nurturing to each individual child.

It is also worth bearing in mind that there are no special receptors in our body for feelings of love or caring. Our eyes, for instance, are a receptor for sight and our ears for hearing but there are no weird antennae for detecting when we are cared for. We can only access that knowledge through our five senses. (Yes, I am aware that in child development there are actually eight senses and counting but for now we are focusing on the five!)

Image 1.2   A person with special antennae for love and caring by M

Do we know we are cared for?

I have occasionally found myself working with abusive parents. Some parents in this situation can still believe that they care for their children. However, does the child know they are cared for when every one of their five senses is telling them they are worthless? The simple truth is that they don't.

So, it is not enough for children to be cared for, they must fundamentally *know* that they are cared for. They can only do this through the evidence of their five senses. The difficulty is that all children are different. What is perceived as nurturing for one child might be a source of stress to another. I know I don't like hugging strangers, but I love a hug from my family (see, I'm not a monster after all!). I work with some children for whom eye contact lets them know that they are important to me. For other children eye contact can be seen as threatening and a source of anxiety. Every child is different and will need nurturing in different ways.

An absence of smiles

A smile is one of the most basic and fundamental nurturing methods. A simple smile can make all the difference and is something that even very young babies respond to. In fact, babies' eyesight has such a short focal distance when they are born that focusing on the smiling face of a loving carer is a vital early nurturing experience. Now think of a post-pandemic world where a generation of young children have seen less smiles because a majority of people have been wearing face masks. On our adoption activity days when masks were still being worn, we told all of our workers and adopters to '*Make sure your smile reaches your eyes!*'

A smile is even more important to our vulnerable children because it tells the child two very crucial things. One, they are safe and two, they are liked. These two simple concepts are profoundly important and until the child feels fundamentally safe and liked they will struggle to thrive. The problem is that in times of stress and anxiety we are all less inclined to smile and so this vital aspect of nurturing can be neglected. It is one of the simplest ways in which we express nurturing and perhaps the easiest to forget and yet the smile is a fundamental aspect of well-being.

Back to the biochemistry – Endorphins

We have all heard of endorphins. These are 'feel good' chemicals that have pain release properties and are produced in our pituitary gland. You may have heard of runners describing an 'endorphin rush' whilst running and this is exactly what is happening. The pituitary gland produces endorphins in response to pleasure stimuli such as food and sex and in response to pain to help alleviate the pain. The difference between endorphins and dopamine, going back to the running analogy, is that dopamine is produced as a reward for crossing the finish line whereas endorphins are the feeling of euphoria during the race itself. Just in case this feeling of euphoria whilst running is sounding a little dubious to many of you, the interesting thing is that you only produce endorphins if you are enjoying the running (or other physical activity). If like me, you hate every single step of a run, you are not alone and you are also unlikely to be producing endorphins. So why do some people love running and produce endorphins whilst a significantly higher proportion of people do not? Well one theory is to do with how our brains are conditioned to view physical activity when we are children. If we are encouraged to take part, enjoy and feel successful at physical activity, then we are more likely to keep those feelings into adulthood. If, however, our childhood experiences of physical activity are negative, make us feel like failures and ultimately make us disengage, we are much less likely to produce those feel-good chemicals and are likely to produce stress hormones instead.

Image 1.3   Two people running: one loves it, the other hates it! By Emily

Endorphins are another key chemical when looking at life-long well-being, actively reducing stress and alleviating symptoms of depression. There seems to be a strong correlation between endorphin production and mental health and even improving sleep. The production of endorphins has been linked to self-esteem, a key component in confidence and well-being, and has even been attributed to sharpening memory and concentration, which enhances learning and development for our children.

So how do we produce more endorphins? Well, one important way to increase these biochemicals is through laughter and I have certainly seen first-hand that settings full of laughter often have thriving children. Enjoying music has also been shown to produce endorphins, as has singing, dancing and even taking part in art or creativity. In fact, I have been so blown away with the benefits of singing that I have begun singing on my courses (much to everyone's regret) and have dedicated an entire section of this book purely to the benefits of singing and music.

Was it me?

I was getting ready to teach a session in a baby room recently and there was a baby left over whose parents were late collecting them. As I set up, I heard the baby room worker singing to the baby, 'Somebody's pooed their nappy now...' I thought to myself, there's only two other people in the room: myself, and the baby, so I hope to God she is not referring to me! The joyful exchange of music over something simple and mundane like a poo-filled nappy was a wonderful, shared moment of attunement play and the absolute opposite of adults who sound actively cross or flustered when a baby soils their nappy.

We also produce endorphins as a way of reducing pain and one interesting suggestion is that we produce endorphins when we eat spicy food such as a curry because the spicy sensation tricks the brain into thinking we are in pain. Pharmaceutical companies are actually using this by adding curcumin (a component of chillies) to pain relief medication. Again, you have to actually enjoy spicy food for this to happen. If curry is not your cup of tea, then how about chocolate? (Now I've got you interested!) Dark chocolate has been shown to potentially increase the production of endorphins and even improve cognitive performance. The downside to this is that most commercially available chocolates have very little actual cocoa in them and large amounts of sugar and fat.

A road map for a joyful childhood

So, we now have a whole series of chemicals that would seem to be intrinsically linked to feelings of happiness, reward and emotional safety and we know to some degree what kind of experiences children need to have to be able to produce these chemicals. However, there is more than just neuro-transmitters at play here. In my previous book I looked at three systems in the brain that signified for me a road map and pedagogy for working with vulnerable children.

In Jaak Panksepp's book, *The Archaeology of Mind* (Panksepp & Biven, 2012), he proposes a series of 'emotional behaviours' in the primitive parts of our brain that we share with all mammals. Three of these, the pro-social emotions, are the basis for all of my work with children. Play, curiosity and nurturing are the fundamental approaches to our work, and I have seen time and time again how profound these three concepts are to the well-being and development of our children. Jaak identified these three instincts as being in the same part of the brain as food, sex and sleep with corresponding powerful biochemicals. These biochemicals are potent drugs that actually have a street value and are as powerful as prescription grade medication. This means that when children play in a stimulating, enriched environment and feel fundamentally safe and cared for, they will produce an entire cocktail of prescription grade drugs that make them feel amazing. At the same time as producing these potent biochem-icals they will also be producing copious quantities of dopamine, serotonin and oxytocin, not to mention being flooded with endorphins. What we are looking at here is the optimum biochemicals for well-being.

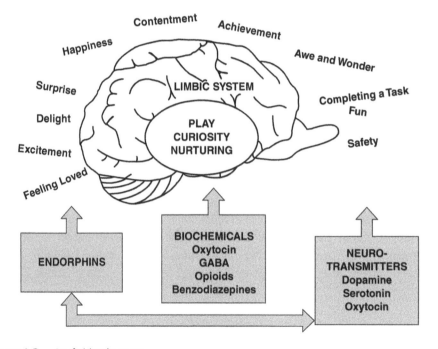

Figure 1.2   Joyful brain map

So, what does this look like in practice?

If we accept that joy is an important part of every childhood, then we now have a series of clearly defined experiences for our children which will enable them to have the most fulfilling and joyful childhood possible. Looking at the biochemicals of joy we can see exactly which experiences are likely to produce these chemicals. Using the three aspects of joy we can create experiences for children to help them thrive.

Nurturing and feeling safe

Before any progress can be made the child MUST feel safe, secure and nurtured. This has to be the platform for every other aspect of learning, development and well-being. We will discuss this later in the book, but feelings of anxiety, shame, humiliation and fear will effectively reduce the child's capacity to learn and critically undermine their emotional well-being. From the moment a child enters the setting they must feel fundamentally valued, important and loved.

We need to acknowledge that children's experiences outside of our setting may have led to them feeling anything but emotionally safe and that we may need to be extremely proactive in supporting our children. They need to know at the deepest of levels and from the earliest of ages that we have their backs, and we will protect them.

The rope swing of doom

Several years ago, I worked with a group of children who had severe behavioural conditions and had extremely negative experiences of childhood. Lorenzo, who had been looked after by a series of foster carers really struggled with his relationship with adults, for obvious reasons. He treated me just as he did all other adults, with a mixture of fear, anger and outright hostility. Every time I spoke to him, he would swear at me and if he referred to me at all it was with a particularly unpleasant word which I will leave up to your imagination. Whilst on a rope swing over a stream, Lorenzo lost momentum and became stuck. He was hanging desperately over the water and for the first time he actually used my name when he cried, 'Ben – please help me!'. Now, I am uncomfortable with being called a hero but if you insist. I strode into the water, muscles rippling (or sagging), picked Lorenzo up and carried him from the stream. In fairness, the water was only about two inches deep and he was never in any real danger of anything but wet toes. The thing is that what had been a throwaway gesture to me was actually a pretty big deal to Lorenzo. From that moment he stopped calling me names and actually began to join in with all the activities planned. He even helped me load up the van afterwards. I think the simple fact that an adult had his back when he needed it was profoundly important and, for a child such as Lorenzo, incredibly rare.

We also need to acknowledge the fact that children are nurtured in very different ways and that what works for one child will not necessarily work for another. In the current post-pandemic world, I believe it is no longer enough to just assume that our children feel nurtured. Remember that we only have five senses for information to enter our brains, so we need to make sure that the simple message of caring gets into each and every child's brain through their five senses. If we assume a child is cared for without ensuring they *know* they are cared for then it is the equivalent of not being cared for at all. Rather than asking how do we make sure our children feel cared for, we need to ask specifically how do we make sure Rhizwan feels cared for, how do we make sure Isobel feels cared for, Felix, Ahmed, Danielle, etc. In short, we need to tailor our nurturing to meet the needs of each individual child through their five senses. We need to discuss our children's nurturing needs as an ongoing aspect of our reflective practice and regularly reassess whether our children feel fundamentally safe, cared for, important and loved.

Five senses of nurturing

Sight

- Smiles (make sure they reach your eyes)
- Showing interest in the child and their world
- Facial expressions whilst reading or telling stories
- Open, welcoming body language (being on a child's level, open arms, etc)
- Shared visual experiences looking at pictures, photos or even the clouds together

Sound

- Soothing tone of voice
- Friendly words
- Never crossing the line between firm and mean
- Laughter
- Praise
- Singing and music

Touch

- Hugs (if appropriate to the child)
- Reassuring touches, pats on the shoulder, etc

- Providing and sharing sensory play

- Dancing together

- Rough and tumble play

- Holding hands

Taste

- Enjoying food together – adults sitting with the children during food time (remember the family meal around a table is declining so this can also be a vital social experience)

- Tasting new foods

- Cooking and baking together

Smell

- Familiar smells – a blanket from home to support children to feel safe

- Consistent smells – if you wear the same perfume or use the same shampoo on a daily basis then changing this can cause moments of dissonance, especially for our youngest children

- Avoiding overpowering or unpleasant smells

- Sharing sensory play together

Bespoke sensory nurturing

Some children will find strong sensory input to be upsetting and some will crave strong sensory input. We therefore need to tailor our nurturing to each individual child if we are to ensure they feel fundamentally safe and cared for in our settings.

Experience is key

Once the child feels safe and nurtured in our presence we can really go to town on the joyful experiences. Children need to feel happiness and contentment, they need to achieve and feel successful and they need moments of surprise, awe and wonder.

It is worth bearing in mind that brain growth is experiential. This means that the mushy unformed brains of babies, that are only 30 per cent (ish) of the size of an adult's brain, need experiences to grow to their full size and potential. More important than genetics, more important than natural stages of development, the brain needs experiences to grow. Put simply, a childhood full of rich, joyful experiences will grow the brain in a very different way to a childhood full of anxiety. Remember that experiences fundamentally shape the architecture of the brain for the rest of the child's life and so giving a broad range of joyful experiences is the best possible start in life for any child.

In addition, the broad range of biochemicals produced through joyful experiences are the optimum biochemicals for happiness and well-being, combatting anxiety and depression, improving memory and cognition and intrinsically linked to confidence and self-esteem. Knowing all this, the question should not be *how* can we make sure every child experiences a joyful childhood but rather *why* do we not ensure that every single child experiences joy?

Clowning around

So, I do have a bit of a problem with clowns. It is not the phobia that some people describe, especially having watched the film, *It*. No, my experience of clowns has been negative because the humour they display is occasionally at the expense of children. Many years ago, we hired a clown for a summer play scheme and whilst it all started well it appeared that all of the 'funny' jokes were at the expense of the children. One example was a magic trick the clown performed where, because he was a clown, everything went wrong. This should be a funny idea, but the humour was lost because all the things that went wrong were the fault of his assistant who was a child he had picked from the audience. He handed the child a wand, it instantly went floppy; he handed the child a top hat, it collapsed, and a toy rabbit fell out of it. He handed the child a spotty handkerchief and all the spots fell off. He kept repeatedly berating the child for doing it wrong even though that was part of the act in the first place. Now some of you won't see the harm in this but the child he had picked had experienced extreme neglect, including starvation, before being adopted. The clown finished by giving the child a Mars bar in a bag which kept vanishing whenever he handed the bag to the child. This is not joy! Yes, there was laughter but certainly not from the young boy who was close to tears. Since then, I have encountered clowns who seem to actually despise children, clowns who are rude and aggressive and even a clown who told dirty jokes in front of the children. Maybe I just have bad luck with clowns?

So, throughout this book we are looking at the amazing people who bring joy to their children, the people who go above and beyond in their pursuit of joy and who stand up for their children's right to joy in their lives. But lurking in the shadows are the clowns, the people who without a thought, fundamentally remove the joy from children.

Summary

So, joy is a big deal, often neglected, but a vital aspect of every childhood. It is a unique and powerful feeling, transcending barriers and creating magic. It encompasses feelings of happiness and contentment with stimulation and engagement, and must be underpinned by feelings of safety, security and feeling valued and cared for. It produces an entire cocktail of biochemicals which are the optimum biochemicals for well-being. And we absolutely must do whatever we can to ensure our children experience joy because we only get one chance at a childhood and a childhood without joy is potentially a childhood full of fear and anxiety.

2
THE JOY OF GOO AND BIG RED BUSES!

Here there be dragons

You've probably all seen a bus before. Most of us, if we are honest, are not that impressed by buses, having seen hundreds if not thousands over the course of our lives. Sometimes though, we need to try to see the world through the eyes of a child. Imagine a young child seeing a big red bus for the first time. Imagine just how enormous the bus would seem to the child, how noisy its engine and how the smell of diesel fills the air as it thunders past. No fire breathing dragon from stories could ever be so magnificent and awe inspiring. Yet, as an adult, we hurry the child away because we are late, it's raining, and we no longer believe in dragons. Our adult tendency to take the magical and make it mundane is the opposite of the child's innate sense of joy at the unknown, the new and the amazing.

Image 2.1   A cross between a bus and a dragon by R

A sensory buffet

You will have noticed I did not just describe how the bus looked but also how it smelled and the noise it made. There would also be the feeling of the vibrations as it rumbled past. This is because to children the world is a sensory buffet, and their senses are constantly alive and questing for information. For adults, sight is our primary sense with sound a close second, but very young children are much more keyed into their other senses. Babies will try to put anything they can into their mouths because taste is an important way in which they explore their world. The sense of touch is also a key exploratory behaviour hence the fact that young children touch everything, squish everything and stick their fingers in everything.

Back to joy

So how does this link in with our concept of joy? Well, in addition to happiness we need elements of engagement and stimulation. The joy of exploring and discovering new sights, sounds, tastes, feelings and smells is the very essence of sensory play. What children are doing when they make those sensory explorations is fundamentally learning about their world. They are also making vital connections and building up the experiences that help them to understand their own place in the world and how to navigate it safely.

Not just for young children

There seems to be a belief that sensory play is just for very young children, but we use it with all ages and it can be just as effective with a 9-year-old (or even a 14-year-old) as with a 3-year-old.

Exploring curiosity

We explored the concept of curiosity in my previous book. According to Jaak Panksepp, curiosity is a limbic system response in the same part of the brain as food and sex and sleep. This means it floods the brain with a whole range of biochemicals in exactly the same way as when we eat cake. In fact, as taste is a primary exploratory system, eating cake also counts as sensory play. Remember as adults we have a solemn duty to give our children positive experiences of childhood, which means copious amounts of research. This means you should go and eat some cake right now, purely as research into sensory play.

Now that you've finished your cake, activating the curiosity system floods the brain with positive biochemicals, makes the child feel amazing and ensures the behaviour is repeated so the child better understands their world. Many of the chemicals associated with this part of the brain are addictive (opioids, benzodiazepines) which means the child craves sensory stimulation. Therefore, any learning opportunity stimulating the basic curiosity system also leads to the child wanting more of that learning. So, the simple joy of exploring with each of the five senses is profoundly important for the child's emotional well-being and also impacts on their innate desire for learning. These experiences are also incredibly neurologically rich. Once again, the brain can only access the world through the senses. Or more accurately, the world can only effect the brain through the senses. This means that every bit of experiential brain development is reliant on the senses because it cannot take place in any other way. Play that stimulates multiple senses, activating the curiosity system, is therefore a vital way in which children grow their brains.

Cognitive disequilibrium

Bernadette Duffy takes this a step further when she equates messy play with Piaget's concept of cognitive disequilibrium. In essence, changes in external stimuli, accessed through the senses, make the child change their mindset to meet the new situation (Duffy, 2004, 2007).

The limbic system is sometimes called the paleo mammalian cortex or simply the mammal brain because it is shared with all mammals. This part of the brain is arguably about 200,000,000 years old and you can easily see the parallels between how human children play and explore and how dogs, cats, rats and mice play and explore. With the exception of humans this is pretty much as far as it goes. The simple joy of a dog finding a particularly interesting stick or smelling a particularly unpleasant smell is as far as animals take this primitive system.

The smartest monkey

In humans there is more though. There is a whole world of curiosity that transcends the primitive parts of our brain and unlocks the uniquely human and very special parts of our brain. There is a huge difference between sticking a crayon in your mouth because you like the taste and feel of it, and wanting to know the names of every dinosaur and/or tank engine because you are fascinated by dinosaurs and tank engines. The conscious, self-aware part of our brain that finds facts, figures and concepts fascinating is far from the primitive instinctive limbic system. Let's face it, our dogs and cats are never mesmerised by a beautiful sunset or stare at the sky imagining pictures in the clouds.

Pebble hunting

You can see this conscious curiosity in your children. I quite often hide resources such as shiny rocks, pebbles and fossils for young children to 'discover'. All mammals explore and forage and children will love hunting for the interesting items and resources in the same way. A dog will find and bring back random items just as a human child does. The difference is that only a human child starts to categorise and quantify the exploratory objects. A child will bring back one random white rock, for instance, and then start hunting for other white rocks. Or, when they bring a selection of rocks back, they will begin to sort and quantify, exploring the similarities and differences between the items and making connections. This unique behaviour is the conscious aspect of curiosity in action: the capacity of humans to find things stimulating, not just on an instinctive level but on a conscious one.

So, the next time you watch an interesting documentary it is the uniquely human part of your brain that is stimulated. If you are eating cake at the same time, then your limbic system will also be active. If it happens to be a documentary about cake, then it is a double whammy.

Working with children, we need to provide the wonderful instinctive sensory explorations and messy play that creates a limbic system response. We also need to feed the innate and uniquely human aspect of curiosity that makes children fascinated in finding out about their world on a conscious level. The reward system is once again at play here. Finding out something that genuinely interests us gives us a tiny hit of dopamine. Finding someone to share this with gives us a hit of oxytocin. The human desire to make connections between different things and concepts gives a sense of achievement and activates the reward system. Ultimately it is those connections that expand human knowledge. However, if the child explores something new and surprising it is even more powerful.

What's in the box?

I occasionally receive donations from companies so imagine my excitement when on the morning before a visit to a school I received a cardboard box full of den making material. I did not have time to open the box so I just shoved it in the van and set off for the session. At the beginning of the session, which was working with children struggling with low confidence, I handed the children the box to see what was inside. I cannot describe the infectious excitement which occurred as the children opened up the box and pulled out the brightly coloured materials one by one. Even though I already had a rough idea of what was in the box, I became more and more thrilled by each shiny bit of material as the children, 'oohed' and 'aahed' as if watching the most entrancing firework display. The sad fact is that it would never have occurred to me to give the children the unopened box if I had not been so short of time in the morning. I would have unpacked the material myself and put it in the den making kit bag ready for the children. The joy of discovery simply would not have happened.

So, it turns out that there is potentially a biochemical reason for this joy of discovery. Dopamine production is significantly increased when we experience surprising or unexpected happiness. The little boy who had not realised the potion would light up or the underconfident children who were entranced by the succession of shiny bits of material, had potentially experienced increased dopamine production because the experience was unexpected. This brings us right back to awe and wonder as intrinsically important, not merely for learning and development but because they increase the production of dopamine and are a key component of joy.

Awe and wonder

Awe and wonder are crucial to the life experiences of a child. Put simply, awe and wonder are the joy at discovering the innate amazingness in a child's world, whether this is a big red bus or seeing a rainbow for the first time. It is vitally important that we not only support our children to experience this amazingness but also recognise just how special things can be if we allow children to experience the world without the preconceptions and prejudices of adulthood. Case in point is a rainy day. Watching families in the rain you will often see the 3-year-old looking up with joy and experiencing the rain on their faces. Chances are their carers will be frowning and hurrying along, expressing the frustration and stress of a rainy day. Eventually the child will begin to see the rain as adults do, which is an unpleasant inconvenience rather than the genuine miracle it truly is.

The robots are coming: Part one

We often build giant robots out of cardboard. We build them in stages with groups of children working on each section and then assembling the robot bit by bit. The weird thing is that even though it should be obvious how big the eventual robot is going to be by looking at the component parts, the children are always absolutely astounded at how big the robot actually is. Awe and wonder – job done!

Image 2.2 Cardboard robot

I often meet early years practitioners and playworkers who are the opposite of the cynical unimpressed adults. They are excited by the shiny materials I use on my training courses and they audibly 'ooh' at the light up potions. They race around on scooter boards during the practical sections or create the most amazing things out of cardboard. I really don't know how to say this but in other areas of society these people's behaviour could be considered weird. Yet as professionals working with children these people (you know who you are) are invaluable. They have managed to hold on to their joy in the world and are now able to pass that joy on to their children. Their attitude, more than anything, is promoting the very awe and wonder that we know is so important to our children's development.

Super powered ballet dancers

I play a very simple superhero game where we shout out super powers and then children pretend they have those powers. I shout things like, 'superspeed', 'flying' and 'super strength' and the children behave as if they have those powers, usually whilst running around laughing. (See, I said it was simple.) When I do this activity with adult training groups, I throw in some slightly unusual powers just to see what the group will do. I quite often shout things like, 'ballet dancing powers'. Many adults when confronted by something that clearly does not fall within the expected parameters of a game or activity would do nothing. There are some people however, who instantly start ballet dancing. These are the people who show joy to their children.

The truth is though, that we are not all like this. For some of us the struggles of adult life have led us to become world weary and cynical and increasingly unable to see joy in simple things. Others feel that we don't have the confidence to express ourselves in this way. Does this mean we can't inspire joy in our children? The answer is emphatically 'no'. It does not matter how underconfident, exhausted or old we feel, we can still acknowledge the wonder in a child's world and help them to experience it.

A fundamental belief that nothing is impossible

I briefly mentioned this in my previous book, but I want to reiterate. Working with children you can achieve the impossible, and we are only limited by our imagination, which according to Einstein is limitless. Using imagination and some cardboard boxes you can build a submarine and visit the bottom of the ocean, invent a machine that turns children into dinosaurs or fly into space in a rocket.

These are experiences that in the real world would be impossible but with imagination they become not only possible but a source of joy for our children.

Image 2.3   A machine turning children into dinosaurs by R

One thing that might help is to remember that children are much more engaged in the process of doing something than in a perceived goal. This means that so long as something is fun and engaging it really doesn't matter if it succeeds in any conventional meaning of the word. Basically, you can try lots of things with children and just have fun with it and if it doesn't work you can try something new.

Ben the aero engineer

Several years ago, I worked at a setting which had a climbing tower. This was an ideal place to launch paper aeroplanes from and so we had a lovely summer afternoon making and launching paper aeroplanes. The next day one child asked, 'Can I make a giant paper aeroplane?' I replied that we had some A3 paper which would make it bigger. 'No Ben, I said a giant paper aeroplane'. I dutifully found some A2 paper for the child. 'No Ben, I said a GIANT paper aeroplane!' There then followed almost two days of taping pieces of paper together, with the help of several other children, until we had a single sheet of paper about four metres long. We then folded this into a basic paper dart which was far too floppy to carry let alone fly. Another child suggested we reinforce the plane with bamboo canes and even more tape, so we did. Eventually we had an aeroplane that was absolutely gigantic, so we decided to launch it from the tower. This is when we realised, we had made the plane Indoors and it would not fit through the door. We had to dismantle the plane and remake it outdoors. It took over twenty children to carry the aeroplane and get it into position on the tower for its first flight. Did it fly majestically, gliding across the playground in a glorious moment of transcendent beauty? No, of course it didn't. It plummeted straight down and smashed into a hundred pieces of splintered bamboo and torn paper. It turns out that aero engineering is not as easy as you may think. The thing is, nobody felt disappointed. It had been such an epic thing to attempt that even though it failed, we all felt that we had done something genuinely amazing.

Cultural capital

I also believe the idea that nothing is impossible is a fundamental aspect of cultural capital. Raising the aspirations of young children is vital for their eventual success and part of cultural capital is clearly empowering and supporting children with new experiences and broadening their knowledge of the world. Another crucial element is supporting them to see the possibilities inherent in their world and what can be achieved with a little imagination.

The superhero head teacher

Dave McPartlin is a head teacher who takes this to the next level by not only discussing the dreams and aspirations of his children but by actually making them happen. Through perseverance and imagination, he has created the most incredible experiences for his children with memories that will last their lifetimes. He arranged for some of his children to drive sports cars and one girl got to meet a 'real' unicorn. Yes, it was a horse with a horn stuck on its head but what an incredible memory for that child. His most famous achievement was to get his children through to the semi-finals of *Britain's Got Talent* because it was one girl's dream to be on the show. If you have not watched the Youtube video of this, I urge you to as it is incredibly moving. His children have had the most unique experiences which would not have happened if one adult had not taken a stand and refused to admit the impossible.

Back to joy. So, our initial concept of joy is intrinsically bound up with the concepts of surprise, amazement and awe and wonder and this in turn supports cultural capital by raising children's aspirations and showing them the possibilities that exist in the world. The joy of completing or succeeding produces dopamine but this should be on the child's terms, not the adults and their success criteria can be very different to an adult's. Remember, the fact that the aeroplane did not fly did not stop the experience being incredibly rewarding.

Winter Olympics

One year we were asking children what themes they would like over our summer play scheme. A young boy said, 'We did Olympics last year so why don't we do winter Olympics this year?' A member of staff then said, 'We can't do winter Olympics in the middle of summer!' You've guessed the rest. We did a winter Olympics theme in the middle of summer. We made toboggans out of cardboard (with the children's legs poking out of the bottom). We made cardboard skis,

(Continued)

taped them to our shoes and jumped off a hill for the ski jump. We also used the water slide for figure skating and curling (frozen plastic milk bottles were used as curling stones because they have handy handles!). Perhaps the weirdest event was the 'see who can melt an ice cube the fastest' competition. One young boy was amazing at this. Rishi may never have won anything in a PE lesson or on sports day, but he had the hottest hands on the planet and for an entire week was treated like an utter legend by the other children.

What does this look like in practice?

Well, first and foremost we need to ensure that our children's lives are full of sensory explorations of their world. Real experiences, as opposed to screen based, will give children far more of the sensory feedback and joy their brains need to understand their world and to grow and develop. We need to create a sensory buffet for our children, allowing and supporting them to experience a broad range of sensory input and experiment and create within those experiences. Keep reminding yourself that the only way we can impact on the child's brain is through their senses. We need to foster that sense of awe and wonder at the amazingness of the world through all of their senses.

Loose parts play and open-ended resources

I mentioned loose parts play at length in my previous book, but I cannot stress how important this kind of play is to our children. This is play that activates the primal curiosity system through physically manipulating and experiencing a wide range of resources. It also simultaneously activates the upper brain of imagination and problem solving through exploring possibilities in the resources. In addition, loose parts play activates the reward system on the child's terms as they are creating and experimenting following their own ideas and instincts rather than the adult's. I also believe there is an enhanced dopamine response as they manipulate interesting resources in new and often surprising ways and if that wasn't enough, they also develop resilience and a growth mindset by using trial and error to achieve their goals.

This is the one type of play I use with all ages and ability levels and if you were to pin me down to just the barest minimum of resources, I would choose old bits of material and cardboard boxes. Old bits of material can be dens, costumes, art, superhero capes, tug of war ropes, hammocks, kites or assorted swirly things. They are clearly visually engaging, but they also have different textures and even different sounds as they swish through the air. I collect old duvets and curtains and then I supplement the material with the odd box of shop bought shiny and special materials (because my children are worth it!). Cardboard boxes are also incredibly versatile. They can be hats, cars (*Flintstones* style with the legs sticking out), dens, castles, tunnels, boats, Aztec pyramids or simply a safe space to sit and chat. Put on top of scooter boards they can be a chariot, a car, or a train. The best bit about loose parts play and open-ended resources is that children, rather than passively experiencing the amazingness in the world, actually create their own amazingness, flooding their brains with dopamine.

More unexpected joy

During one session with young children with profound and multiple learning disabilities we got the bag of material out so they could explore the various sights and textures. The children loved rubbing the material on their faces to feel the different textures. One girl began draping the material over her head and giggling. We happened to have some mirrors handy so we gave them to the children so they could see themselves with the material on their heads. It is very difficult to describe the absolute joy that ensued as the children tried the different bits of material on their heads and giggled out loud. The next week we tried it with different coloured wigs!

The mystery of Marmite

Remember that the enemy of loose parts play is '*That's not supposed to be used for that!*' If humanity had never used things in ways they were not supposed to be used, then we would never have invented fire, the wheel or marmite! Often the whole point of loose parts play is to use items in a variety of different ways, none of which are their intended use. Our cardboard boxes were never designed to be space rockets, for instance.

I think that another way we undermine joy is making everything too adult and slavishly sticking to the rules. Many older people will remember the best childhood games were the ones we made up and the rules were constantly changing to fit the circumstances. Never be afraid to throw out the rules and make up something new. If something is not working then rather than continuing, change it up and try something new.

How to fail your driving test

I worked with a setting once who said they occasionally play 'traffic lights'. This is the game where if you shout 'green light' the children run, shout 'red light' and

(Continued)

they stop, and if you shout 'amber light' they crawl on all fours. The practitioner said that the children would quickly get bored of this (and who wouldn't?). I suggested that they add other lights such as 'purple light' which means 'pull a funny face'. The practitioner looked at me in bewilderment and said, 'but traffic lights don't have purple lights.' I am pretty sure we don't need to be worried about an accurate depiction of the Highway Code when working with 6-year-olds. I can't imagine a future time where an 18-year-old fails their driving test because they once played a game with different coloured traffic lights. 'Sorry I didn't stop at the red light, I thought it was a purple light' (whilst pulling a funny face).

Sometimes to give children those new and surprising experiences we need to throw the rule book out and just make stuff up. Not only are you inspiring joy but also supporting a mindset of creative problem solving.

The mystery of Marmite: Part two

On the subject of creative problem-solving, Marmite is an interesting one. Marmite is a product of the brewing industry and was discovered by accident. Strangely, no one previously had thought to put the strange black goo in their mouths because, let's face it, that's just weird. And yet now millions of people enjoy it (or hate it) on toast.

Surprise

We know that surprising happiness increases dopamine. Receiving your monthly wages may make you happy but that is nothing compared to the happiness felt when you find a tenner in the bottom of your jeans pocket that you didn't realise was there. So, let's ensure children experience the tenner in the pocket feeling not just the ordinary wages feeling. Have plenty of things for children to discover and find for themselves. Bring in boxes with unknown contents: will it be shells, will it be gold coins, will it be slugs? Let children unbox resources, open parcels and find buried treasure. Bury dinosaurs in the sandpit. Bring in ornaments from faraway lands or wonderful new foods to try.

We also need to put ourselves in the mind of a child. Remember the first time we ever saw or experienced something new. Most of us find it hard to really remember just how exciting the world was when we were children.

Fresh snow, fresh eyes

I had a friend who moved to the UK from Malaysia when he was 16. I was standing next to him when it snowed. He had never seen snow except on TV before and even all these years later I will never forget the joy on his face as he saw and felt the snow for the first time.

We all know that bubbles pop, right? But just imagine for a second that we didn't. We know all about spherical objects, we have seen and played with balls and eaten oranges and none of those popped. If you didn't already know a bubble was going to pop there would be no indication at all that this was going to happen, after all why would it? And then it pops! A tiny moment of disequilibrium where we adjust our sense of reality to meet the new observations. Also though, a tiny moment of joy, an enhanced rush of dopamine and an overwhelming desire not just to see more bubbles but make them pop yourself. Then of course the surprise of tasting soap when you inevitably try to eat one. This is what I am talking about. If we can give children experiences that are as amazing as the first pop of a bubble, then we are bringing joy to a child. When we propagate to children our adult sense of the world as dull and unsurprising all we do is lessen the amount of joy.

Unique art

One setting decided when it snowed not merely to make snow people but to actually paint them! I have honestly never thought to do this before but what a lovely idea. Then when the snow people melt there is a little pool of colour left on the ground. I love it when settings do something so creative that very few people would even think to do it.

I believe there are some experiences that transcend that 'first-time' joy and surprise. When the potions light up the children are not just enthralled for the first potion, but again and again as the different coloured potions light up. When we see a firework display, we 'ooh' and 'aaah' throughout the display even though we may have seen many fireworks before. Bubbles popping engage children long after that initial moment of surprise. We need to find those magical experiences and share them with our children.

A big TV

Many, many years ago I was a babysitter for two young children. They lived on Coventry Road, their nursery and school were on Coventry Road, the shops and park were on Coventry Road and in fact every single part of their lives took place on Coventry Road. They had never been on holiday and not had a single experience that had not taken place on Coventry Road. When I first met them, they even asked me where on Coventry Road I lived. I decided one day to take them to the cinema. Having no experience of the cinema, Jamie's mum had told him that it was like a big television. When we walked in and he saw the screen he stopped dead in his tracks and just stared, open mouthed at the huge screen. In his wildest dreams he could never have imagined the size of the cinema screen.

Another really useful bit of theory is the fact that imaginary experiences activate the brain in the same way as real-life experiences. One example is that imagining playing the piano improves your actual ability to play the piano. This is so important for working with children. This means that imaginary surprise will still enhance dopamine production. It means that games of pirates or space people can have genuine surprise when the pretend mermaid and/or alien arrives. It means if children are enthralled by a story, then every plot twist or surprising appearance of poo (in the story not actual poo) will give children an enhanced hit of dopamine. The ramifications of this are endless and I know that since learning about this I have paid special attention to those often-overlooked moments of genuine surprise and discovery and in particular how we can use imagination to unlock those feelings in children.

Drums in the deep

Here's a lovely activity for you. We recently worked on an adoption family play event and one little boy decided to make a tunnel out of the cardboard boxes we had supplied. This grew into an entire tunnel system with branching tunnels and even a secret cave at the end. Wherever the cardboard boxes joined and let the light in we covered the join with den making fabric so that the tunnels were properly dark and mysterious. Children could then crawl into the tunnels with torches and find the biscuits we had hidden at various points.

Image 2.4   A cardboard box tunnel system

This is everything I am talking about. The joy of building the tunnels, working together to make something new and exciting and creating amazingness! Then the joy of exploration and imagining we are in a deep dark cave system. The slight fear and excitement of venturing into the unknown, then the joy of discovery and surprise when children find a biscuit, or the tunnel opens up into the secret cave. Then the sense of achievement when you emerge, blinking in the light, victoriously clutching your treasure. Finally, the joy of not just eating a biscuit but eating a magical biscuit that you have personally mined from the bowels of the earth.

All this simple activity took was a few boxes, some material, and adults who didn't say no but let the activity grow organically into something truly magical. So, the key here is not the resources but the adults who support the child's ideas rather than restricting them.

Adults need to not merely allow children to experience joy but inspire curiosity through their own enthusiasm. This is not always easy but even the most cynical of us must begin to see the world through the eyes of a child if we are to avoid crushing their innate curiosity. If we feed children's curiosity it will grow; starve it and it will wither.

A literal windfall

I was driving along in my van once, after my son and I had been to a play session, and a ten pound note flew in through the open window (I kid you not - my son actually caught it!). It may have only been ten pounds, but my son and I still smile when we think of that day! Sadly, I was then stopped by the police for going through a purple light without pulling a funny face.

Also, we need to feed the different types of children's curiosity from the visceral feeling of squidging Play Doh to the fascinating worlds of astronomy or wildlife or sea creatures or whatever interests each individual child (everything I know about sea creatures comes from watching *The Octonauts* with my children!). Nothing will stop a child being interested in something quicker than an adult showing disinterest or belittling their genuine passion. We also need to remember that their interests will be different to ours. You may find dinosaurs incredibly dull, but we must show an interest in our children's passions, even if we need to pretend, if we want to feed that all important curiosity and hunger for learning.

We need to understand that even our youngest children can experience awe and wonder, and we can support them to have unique experiences with a little imagination and a belief that nothing is impossible.

If you have a cohort of children who thrives on experimentation and exploration, flooded with biochemicals that make them crave learning, with mindsets of problem solving and creativity, think not merely of the benefits to the children but to society as a whole!

The mystery of Marmite: Part three

Edward De Bono was a celebrated lateral thinker. This means he could come up with innovative and often unusual solutions to problems. When asked for a solution to the Middle East crisis he suggested Marmite. His reasoning? The Middle Eastern diet is often lacking in the vital mineral zinc. Lack of zinc can lead to more aggressive behaviour. If everyone in the Middle East ate more Marmite, which is high in zinc, there would be less violence. Now whether you think this response is genius or ridiculous you have to admit it is unusual and innovative. Interestingly, De Bono suggested that the obsession with testing in education was preventing a significant number of children from reaching their potential. He suggested a more creative approach to teaching would benefit these children (Fryer, 2021).

Summary

In this chapter we learnt that curiosity is amazing and should be supported and fed if we want our children to experience joy. Curiosity is a broad experience, from the visceral joy of goo to the fascination with sea creatures. We need to feed our children's innate desire for a sensory buffet and also stimulate and support their passions for learning about their world. Surprising joy is even more powerful than expected joy, so we need to give our children the tenner in the pocket feeling or the first bubble pop feeling. This highlights the immense importance of awe and wonder in supporting joy but is also intrinsically linked to life-long learning and cultural capital. We explored the concept that nothing is truly impossible with a little imagination and copious amounts of tape, and we revisited the wonderful world of loose parts play, learning along the way that I am really bad at making aeroplanes. We also learnt that Marmite is amazing, and we should all eat more cake.

Final thought

In my first book I mentioned an adult I met who I had previously worked with as a child. We reminisced about our shared experiences and when recounting the tale of the giant aeroplane his recollections differed from mine in one important way. 'Hey Ben, do you remember the giant paper aeroplane that flew across the playground?' His memory of the event had transformed into one of success despite the very real fact that the plane had crashed spectacularly into the ground.

3
EXPRESSIONS OF JOY — THE JOY OF WORDS AND SOUNDS

The power of cardboard

One of our projects works with children who are selectively mute. I will never forget the child who would speak to us only if she was sitting in a cardboard box. This actually led to other children speaking, when they were in cardboard boxes!

There are lots of benefits to making dens and amongst all the physical, problem solving and creativity benefits there is also an undeniable sense of well-being from simply sitting in a den. When I deliver parent training it is often the first activity I do because I have seen how much calmer and more receptive the group becomes after they have sat in their dens and eaten biscuits. Why this should be the case is not fully understood but there is a clue when we look at how the brain works and there is definitely something calming and therapeutic about being in a den.

So, what has this got to do with communication and language? Well, in this chapter I want to demonstrate that joy is not merely a vital aspect of well-being but is an essential part of every aspect of learning and development. I could choose any element of learning, but I believe communication and language is particularly relevant and something that we know many children are struggling with.

The selectively mute child who can speak when she is in a cardboard box can do this because she now feels safe to do so. The sudden feeling of well-being and joy from being in a cardboard box gives a layer of emotional protection that enables her to speak. I also find that imagination play can have similar results. When we pretend to be pirates or superheroes the children will often speak more confidently because they are an imaginary and more 'powerful' version of themselves. Clearly something about those joyful expressions of play is helping children to communicate better.

Children learn language differently to adults

In order to understand the vital role of joy in developing communication and language we need to unpick how children learn to speak in the first place. If an adult learns a new language, they do so in a very different way to our children. An adult has fully formed the communication and language centres of their brain (of which there are many) and has an existing list of words or a template for their current language(s). So if, for instance, I wanted to learn French (*et pourquoi pas?*) I would need to have fully formed communication and language structures in place in my brain and a template of my original language to compare new words with. In short, I need to know the English word 'cheese' in order to compare the French word *'fromage'* and build up a new vocabulary by comparing English to French. In this instance the emphasis is on the words themselves because we are comparing existing vocabulary with the new vocabulary.

This is not how children learn language for two very simple reasons. Firstly, they have not yet fully built the neurological structures for communication and language and secondly, they don't have an existing vocabulary for comparison. When children first learn language, they are physically creating the neurological structures for speech as they develop and are building their vocabulary, not through comparison but by learning new words from scratch.

This means unlike adult learning the emphasis is not on the words themselves but on 'meaning'. To make matters more difficult, words can radically change meaning depending on context and how they are said. If you approached me at a conference and I said, *'hello'*, whilst smiling, the meaning would be pretty clear. If, however, I said, 'hello' whilst waggling my eyebrows suggestively (I would never do this so please do come and talk to me at conferences!) then the word has a whole new meaning, and a restraining order would shortly follow. All silliness aside, the meaning of words is not always dictated by the word itself but by all the other signals that make up language. In short, language is a jigsaw puzzle made up of many different pieces. Body language, facial expression, tone of voice, inflection, pauses and even eyebrows are as important for discerning meaning as the words themselves.

Joy is the key motivator for language

So how does this fit in with our picture of joy? The simple truth is that there is only one reason why children learn language. Because it is fun. If we want to give children as complete a picture of the jigsaw of language as possible it needs to be full of joy. If our early experiences of language are fun and joyful, then we will want to learn more language. If however our experiences are negative or joy is absent then we simply won't. Remember our initial equation for joy. Happiness and stimulation whilst feeling safe. These are the experiences that develop language, the shared moments of joyful conversation between parent/carer/keyworker and child. The baby says, 'boo' so that you say 'boo' back. This cannot happen with screen-based interactions and certainly can't happen if the adult sharing that moment is disinterested or inexpressive.

I touched upon this little neuroscience nugget in my previous book, but I believe it is the most important fact about learning that every educator needs to know. This simple fact gives us a wonderful, joyful alternative to some of the more negative methods of teaching and learning. It also puts 'joy' at the centre of every single learning opportunity. What is this simple nugget?

Neurons that excite together, wire together!

This is all to do with the neuroscience of neural networks and how our brains begin to make associations. Basically, if we have a really positive experience of learning we begin to create links in our brain (associations) between the positive feelings and the learning itself. These associations strengthen over time and ultimately become hard wired in our brains. A neural network is simply multiple areas of our brains working together. So positive experiences of learning create neural networks associating the learning with feelings of happiness and success (dopamine and serotonin). Over time these associations hard wire into permanent neural networks where the child automatically associates positive feelings with the aspect of learning. This not only improves their capability in the specific learning but creates feelings of anticipation and reward whenever the child repeats the learning, which then creates a desire for more learning.

The opposite situation is where children have negative experiences of learning. This can be because the learning is unrewarding, dull or the child feels like a failure. The child then makes associations not of positive feelings but negative. If these negative experiences of learning are repeated the neural networks of association begin to hard wire, which reduces the child's ability to learn and the child automatically associates negative feelings with the specific aspect of learning, making them want to disengage or avoid.

Put simply, joy in this model of learning is not merely an optional extra but a fundamental building block. If a child experiences joy in learning they will become more capable, have a greater desire to learn and feel amazing whilst they do this!

Babies can't play chess!

So, whilst I love working with babies, they are often pretty rubbish at stuff. You can't play chess with a baby, and they are not the most stimulating conversationalists. There is a very obvious reason for this. Their brains are only a fraction of their eventual adult size and have very few connections. What gives the brain its familiar 'cauliflower' shape is the connections made as they learn and grow. The brain physically changes shape as neurons (brain cells) connect with each other. Once again if we look at the brain like electrical wiring, we begin to see a problem. When those all-important connections are made in a child's brain, there are many gaps where the electricity quite literally leaks out. This means those early connections are less efficient, meaning the baby is less capable. Then something pretty magical happens. The connections in the brain become strengthened the more the child repeats the particular aspect of development. Eventually after much repetition a protein sheaf grows around the chains of neurons effectively insulating it, just like the insulating plastic casing on an electrical wire. This is called the myelin sheath and once this grows there is less leakage which increases the child's capability, which means they can now do stuff much better.

So, in terms of learning and development this means that childhood experiences fundamentally shape the child's brain and if these experiences are repeated the child 'hard wires' those structural changes through the process of myelination. Neurons that excite together, wire together so positive joyful experiences of learning shape the brain in a very different way to negative ones and those experiences ultimately hard wire, creating a brain that is highly capable, hungry for learning and actively seeking development. Or, alternatively, a less capable brain that fears learning and actively avoids it.

Peekaboo!

So repetition is absolutely vital for embedding learning. What makes us want to repeat behaviour? Enjoying it. The more fun and joyful we make a game of 'Peekaboo' for instance, the more the baby wants to repeat the game – and boy do they want to repeat it. This repetition hard wires learning into the brain. If we are not enjoying something we simply don't want to repeat it.

I hope all that made sense because it is of such importance that it can impact on a child's development and aspirations for the rest of their life. Speech and language are so important to a child's life chances and a joyful beginning can set up the brain in a way that is intrinsically linked to life-long learning and a growth mindset. The only way to set up those positive neural networks is through joyful experiences of communication and language.

Babies do not need to know what words mean in order to understand that they can be pleasant or unpleasant. Soothing words, funny noises and songs are a world away from aggressive voices and frustration. The tone of the voice is just as important as the words themselves as positive tone will make the baby want to repeat the words whilst negative tone will have the opposite effect.

There and back again

My son initially struggled with reading and has a diagnosis of Irlen's syndrome. At the age of 7 he was still being sent home reading scheme books aimed at 5-year-olds. His vocabulary and comprehension were tested as being equivalent to a 16-year-old, meaning he was completely disenchanted with books for 5-year-olds. In an attempt to rekindle his love of stories I read *The Hobbit* to him as this is a book that I loved as a child. Anyone who knows *The Hobbit* (or has seen the films) will know that there are 13 dwarves, which obviously need individual voices when reading. Now we come to a bit of a problem. I can only reliably do about three

(Continued)

accents and they all drift unerringly towards Welsh as they progress. This meant that the thirteen dwarves had the most ridiculous sounding voices and were so wildly inconsistent that they were never the same from one reading to the next. None of this mattered. What mattered is that my son experienced a joyful reading of one of my favourite childhood books read with all the passion and enthusiasm of a professional narrator (albeit from Cardiff) but without any of the skill, fluency or consistency. This endeavour took months and was unbelievably hard work, but it made such a difference to my son as he came to look forward to the story every night and became fully invested in this wonderful book. It transformed his previous view of stories as dull and as the last page was finished, he looked at me with wide eyes and asked, 'Are there any more books by Tolkien that you could read to me?' I took one look at his eager face, shining with a fundamental love of stories and adventure and said, 'No, sorry, unfortunately Tolkien never wrote any more stories, such a shame'.

OK, so I didn't actually say that. I spent the next two years reading him *The Lord of the Rings*. One of my treasured memories is reading this book to him whilst camping in the Lake District. Sharing such a wonderful story whilst the sun slowly set is a shared memory we will never forget.

I cannot stress how important a joy of stories is for our children. It is intrinsically linked to empathy and is absolutely vital for developing imagination, creativity and problem solving. It is also the start of a unique and amazing process. If children enjoy listening to stories, they will want to repeat the process. If they repeat the process enough, they may just want to tell their own stories. If they gain a joy of telling stories they may ultimately want to write down those stories. The road to literacy begins not with cue cards, phonics and holding a pen, but with a fundamental joy in the written word through stories.

If music be the food of love…

We are currently experiencing a deficit in children's vocabulary and a general decline in children's communication. This has been made worse for many children by the lack of social experiences during the pandemic. In order to support children in their development, we really need to analyse what is missing from children's experiences. From parent consultations we find that children do not have as many bedtime stories, there is less singing in the home and in fact communication as a whole has declined. In order to support these children, we need to give back the joyful experiences of language that are potentially missing.

All the wrong notes and all in the wrong order

This brings us nicely onto singing. A couple of years ago I was asked by a Local Authority to deliver a series of practical workshops for early years practitioners. As always, I was extremely busy and so I skim read the brief, confident I could deliver anything that was requested. I mean, what could possibly go wrong?

What I hadn't realised in my cursory, and quite frankly lazy, reading of the brief was that one of the sessions was all about music and singing. A practical session all about singing! Now I know what you are thinking. Surely this should be no problem for an accomplished trainer like Ben? Surely Ben must have the voice of an angel and the musical awareness of a classically trained composer? The truth is I am terrible at singing. A musical friend of mine once said that every single note I sang was slightly out of tune. To paraphrase Eric Morecambe, I sing all of the wrong notes *and* all in the wrong order.

The mind–blowing impact of music

This posed a unique problem. I am passionate about giving my learners a hands-on training experience and even more passionate about practitioners being enthusiastic in their interactions with children. However, the thought of singing in front of other people filled me with dread. The only solution was that I was going to have to overcome my reluctance and actually sing as part of the course.

I then began to research music and singing. I had absolutely no idea just how intrinsically important music and singing are for children. To say my mind was blown was an understatement. The neurological, emotional and even health benefits of singing are phenomenal and the fundamental importance of music for our whole species cannot be understated.

This was just what I needed to create what I hoped would be a wonderful, insightful course for the learners, but it also needed to be practical. So, with renewed enthusiasm for singing, I prepared some songs for the session, some old, some made up and I even created a rap about early years to demonstrate how rhythm and rhyme activate short- and long-term memory.

A flashback to the 1980's

Now just in case you think I am a complete stranger to the genre of rap music I should point out that I was actually in a rap band in my youth. Aged twelve I was a founder member of the 'Double C Crew' (this stood for 'Calver Crescent', the street I grew up on!). My friend Pete and I would 'breakdance' on lino and make up raps. Obviously at age twelve we couldn't afford record decks, so we simulated the noise of records scratching by zipping our pencil cases back and forth really fast. My rap name was 'Red Rapping Hood' and my friend Pete called himself, 'Pulsating Pete' (I kid you not!).

My first and last music training

So, I arrived at the venue, my brain full of facts and my heart full of song. The training took place at a local town hall which was not a venue conducive to a relaxed atmosphere, and there were over thirty people booked on the training. I should have known things would go badly when even before the training began not a single person chatted. The group sat in absolute silence waiting for the training to start. With some trepidation I looked down from my lectern and began the session with a simple song.

Silence. Not the blissful silence at the end of a long session with children but the awful, awkward silence of thirty people not joining in with a single song. Every subsequent song was met with the kind of look reserved for that time when you tread on a bug and are trying to work out what kind of insect it was by examining the mangled carcass on your shoe. Except the shoe was the auditorium and I was the dead bug.

Don't do the rap Ben!

How I wish I could go back in time and tell myself, 'Don't do the rap! Everything else has bombed so whatever you do don't do the rap!'

I did the rap. If you have ever seen a middle-aged man rapping to thirty silent ladies for an agonising three minutes, then you may still be feeling the trauma from the experience. I know I am. The session ended as it began. In silence.

Interestingly, a majority of the learners gave the training five stars, and one lady said it was the best training she had ever had. Go figure?

Keep on singing

Now don't get me wrong. My experience of singing in front of adults has never stopped me singing with the vulnerable children I work with. In fact, knowing the science behind it has made me sing even more, albeit tunelessly, with my children. You don't need to be able to sing to give joy through songs and music. If all the wrong notes in all the wrong order are sung with joy and enthusiasm, then nobody cares if you win a prize or scare away crows and it might just change your children's lives.

The vital importance of singing

What was it about music that made me so excited? Well, partly it is the neuroscience. Musical experiences are uniquely powerful for brain growth. Put simply, music in childhood makes our brain grow. A 2016 study at the University of

Southern California's Brain and Creativity Institute found that musical experiences in childhood can actually accelerate brain development (Habibi et al., 2016), particularly in the areas of language acquisition and reading skills. So, it would seem that singing and musical experiences are extremely neurologically rich.

There is also a suggestion that singing is a powerful aerobic exercise and helps build a healthy heart and lungs. Who knew that singing is actually exercise? Remember that we build every aspect of our adult health and well-being in childhood, so singing is brilliant for giving children the best start possible in terms of life-long respiratory health. Now think back to those adults who, like me, do not experience endorphins from physical exercise such as running. Maybe singing is a way in which we can get those all-important endorphins whilst also exercising our heart and lungs? Why not try it now? Stop reading and put one of your favourite tunes on and just sing out loud. Of course, it doesn't matter if you are reading this book on the bus – nobody will mind.

Boris the cow

I would often use puppets with children and my favourite was Boris the cow. I would use Boris in our early years setting and he would sing songs about eating grass (his favourite food obviously). He would sing, 'Do I like fish fingers?' and the children would all shout 'NO!' Then he would sing, 'Do I like biscuits?' Again, 'NO!' Then he would sing 'What do I like?' and then the loudest shout of all, 'GRASS!'

A 6-year-old girl subsequently approached me at the afterschool club, over a year after she had left the early years setting and brought me a handful of grass to give to Boris. The next day I gave her a thank you letter from Boris, signed with a hoof print.

So, in singing and music we have an intrinsically joyful process that underpins huge amounts of development and is also linked to life-long health. It is the impact on communication and language, however, that really makes the mind boggle. It turns out that music is vitally important for children in the development of language in the first place. Singing and musical experiences support children to develop auditory discrimination and phonological awareness, the ability to distinguish between the complex sounds and variations within speech. This ability to distinguish between even very subtle variations in sound is vitally important for the development of complex speech. There is even some speculation that singing and music are so vital for the development of speech that communication and language acquisition is actually dependent on those early musical experiences. This means that music and singing are not an optional extra for childhood but the very mechanism by which we develop complex language in the first place! It also means that if musical experiences are absent from early years then a child is highly likely to be delayed in their speech and language.

And we can take this even further. If musical experiences are so vital to speech that speech is reliant on having those early musical experiences, then it stands to reason that singing must have predated speech in the evolution of humans. This is exactly what some anthropologists propose. Early humans, before the advent of speech, would have made musical notes as a pre-cursor to speech. I just love the image of primitive humans, before we even achieved the ability to speak, wandering around singing to ourselves. In short, jazz hands predate fire!

The first songs were love songs

So, what was the reason for these early musical sounds, to attract a mate? (Not with my singing!) To scare away predators? Well one theory suggests that those early musical notes were an expression of nurturing and love for our family or pack. They were an extension of the soothing noises we make to a baby, that developed into the first music. I think this is a wonderful idea of early humanity. Musical notes being a primal expression of our unique capacity to love, ultimately leading to the complex speech we now have.

Now, I know what you are thinking. This is all mere speculation. How can anyone truly know what actually happened thousands of years ago? Well, for the first time in recorded history I can present evidence that music and dancing predate the advent of fire.

Image 3.1   *Jazz hands dinosaur*

The return of singing

Recently I have been approached by an awesome music agency called Boogie Mites to deliver a session on the neuroscience of music and singing. The best bit about this is that they do all the songs, so I don't have to traumatise the audience. In a final twist to the story, though, I showed them the jazz hands dinosaur and commented that it would make a great idea for a children's song. Sue from Boogie Mites said, 'Well, if you write the lyrics, we'll put it to music'. So that is exactly what I did and there is now a song for children called Jazz Hands Dinosaur! (It is free to download - see Appendix.)

Introducing the portable plaything - rhyming!

OK so we can't talk about early childhood experiences of language without mentioning rhyming. This is another one of those almost throw away concepts that turns out to be radically important for our children. Most people know that rhyming helps to embed concepts in short- and long-term memory. Many of us will forget even quite important things about our lives but will never forget the theme tune to a childhood TV show because the rhythm and rhyme embeds it into our memory pretty much forever. Nursery rhymes, rhyming songs and children's stories are incredibly powerful at embedding concepts in children's memories. There is more to it than this though.

The language specialist Opal Dunn calls rhymes, 'Portable playthings' (Dunn, nd). You need no resources, no space, just you and your voice. She describes a sense of satisfaction when completing a rhyme that gives children a feeling of security. Are you thinking what I'm thinking? A sense of satisfaction from completing a rhyme? Is this the reward system at work producing dopamine when we complete the rhyme? Not only are rhymes portable playthings but tiny moments of completion that activate our reward system and help us produce more dopamine. We crave more dopamine therefore we become more invested in the story or song because we want to hear more of the rhymes. I love the idea that simple rhymes are a tiny doorway into our reward system and make us feel good.

So, rhyming makes us feel happy because of the sense of completion and reward. It engages us because the rhythmic language sweeps us up in the narrative and we want to hear more to get that very unique reward. The sense of emotional security that Opal Dunn describes is the icing on the cake. Happiness, engagement and safety, the basic equation for joy apparent in the rhymes and songs we share with our children.

What does this look like in practice?

We need to look at those joyful expressions of language that may have been absent from children's lives and make sure we give as many as we can to the children in our care. Screen experiences cannot give the same level of interactivity and responses of simple real-life interactions with real people.

Crucially we need to prioritise joyful experiences and make sure they do not become side-lined or undervalued. Take storytelling for instance. This should not be a throw away moment such as at the end of the day when everyone else is tidying away. Stories should not be an excuse to keep children occupied whilst other tasks are undertaken. In short, we should never be hoovering during story time. (Unless the story is about a hoover.)

Make stories prime time!

The fabulous and flamboyant Neil Griffiths, ex head teacher, play champion and children's author, is a fervent campaigner for stories. He says that stories should be prime time productions full of awe, wonder, silly voices, songs, dances and joyful movement.

I really like Neil's idea that stories should be 'prime time' productions. Stories, both read from a book and made-up, should be an integral part of every child's day, *every* day. Stories should be prepared with seriousness and delivered with silliness. Stories should never become a chore to read because I guarantee they will then become a chore to listen to. Even if, as a practitioner, you have read the story a hundred times before, it must be read with the same enthusiasm as the first time because for some children it will be the first time. Even if the children have also heard the story many times before, the repetition of something they find joyful will help embed those words and concepts in a way that no amount of screen-time ever can.

Remember the three aspects of joy and apply them to your stories. Make them happy, surprising and support the children to feel safe and they will begin to love story time and look forward to it. Make it a genuine surprise when the caterpillar turns into a beautiful butterfly (sorry, spoiler!) because surprising happiness produces more dopamine. Make it dull and unrewarding and the children will quickly lose interest.

Neck ache?

I observed story time in a reception class recently and the teacher sat on a chair whilst the children sat on the floor to listen to the story. The teacher made the story interesting with fantastic use of voices and a genuine infectious enthusiasm. I enjoyed the story enormously, but I was also sitting on a chair. Every one of the children was sitting with their necks craned upwards to see the teacher's face. This meant two things. Firstly, some of the children could not fully see the teachers face as it was partially obscured by the book. This meant that vital aspects of the jigsaw of language (facial expressions, mouth shape, etc) were now missing. Secondly, the children were all sitting in a slightly uncomfortable position which meant that the overall experience would gradually become more unpleasant as the children's necks began to ache.

Talking of uncomfortable positions, I can't sit cross legged on the floor. Now I know you are probably thinking that this is because I am over fifty years old and my legs just don't bend that way, and you would be right. However, I have never been able to sit like this, even from my earliest childhood and I am not alone. My daughter who is incredibly flexible and gymnastic recently told me how brilliant Year 6 is because she doesn't have to sit cross legged on the floor anymore. There are some children who simply don't find this (rather unnatural) position comfortable. Why then, do we insist on all children sitting the same way? When reading a story, we absolutely need our children to be comfortable because if they are not then their engagement with the story is going to be significantly less. Surely that is the important bit? Just like any adult on a training course who finds themselves in an uncomfortable seating position a child who cannot get comfortable will be less happy, less engaged and may even be experiencing pain. What chance does this child have of becoming fully immersed in a story no matter how enthusiastically it is told? (This also applies to children needing a wee – so let your children go to the toilet before story time if they need to!)

Use easily bored children as a barometer for joy!

We need to use the children who are easily bored or who struggle with attention as a barometer for our stories (and indeed all teaching). If their faces are disinterested or if they are glancing around seeking alternative stimulation, we know we need to change things. If we see their attention wandering, we need to instantly switch it up, add actions to the story, do silly voices or get the children to join in with the story. If we can keep that one child fully engrossed in a story, then it is a safe bet all of the children will be similarly engaged.

What's going on in here?

I recently worked in a school delivering training for midday supervisors on improving play at lunchtimes. As part of the project, I also did a consultation with

(Continued)

children to find out what they needed to make lunchtimes as fun and rewarding as possible. I said to the head teacher, 'I don't want to work with the well-behaved school council children, because they always have these kinds of opportunities. I want ordinary children who wouldn't normally get a chance to work with a consultant'. This instruction was interpreted by the individual class teachers as, 'Send Ben your "naughtiest" children'. I therefore worked with fifteen children who had been handpicked due to their 'challenging' behaviour. We had the best afternoon ever!

Enter Melody, a child, who was so energetic and whose attention flitted from one thing to the next so quickly I knew this was going to be a challenge. I knew I needed to up my game, I needed to be more enthusiastic, more playful and more interesting than any other teacher she had encountered just to get the smallest amount of work from her. And I tried, I really tried and just when I thought I was pulling it off, Melody stood up and walked out of the room. Before I could stop her, she went into the next classroom where a violin lesson was going on, sat down in front of the violin teacher and said, 'What's going on in here then?'

I would not describe Melody's behaviour as negative. She was simply curious and actively conveying a message. Her behaviour, like all behaviour, was communication and what she was communicating to me was, 'You are a boring old fart and I've had enough of you!'

Unfortunately, the violin teacher did see her behaviour as negative and began shouting at her. At this point I had to step in and explain that Melody had done nothing wrong and was merely curious. I further added that in fact it was my fault and if the teacher was going to shout at anybody, he should shout at me. Of course, he didn't.

Once I got Melody back in the room, I tried my best to engage her, finding her most stimulated by loose parts play, and then snuck in consultation questions throughout her play. She turned out to have incredible insight into the lunchtimes and came up with some really vibrant and innovative ideas. I was exhausted afterwards though.

So, the takeaway is to find that one child who is looking out of the window when you are telling stories or teaching and be so vibrant and interactive, they can't help but be enthralled. Use those children as your guide and whilst you might not succeed every time, more times than not, you will have created a magical experience for your children. Sometimes engaging our children can be really hard work but just like with Melody, it's worth the effort.

Sing more

It sounds obvious but when you examine the benefits of musical experiences it is a no brainer. We need to sing more with our children. Not only is it neurologically rich and a great aerobic exercise but it also represents a joyful experience of communication and language that is of paramount importance to children as they develop.

Make sure there are musical experiences aplenty for our children. Plenty of instruments, both improvised and real, need to be available and children need time and space to make their own music. They need to be allowed to hum to themselves and make noises. Adults also need to sing, dance and be musical with children. Find out what music your children hear in the home and play it in the setting, expanding children's musical repertoire and maybe making them feel more at home in the setting.

Singing in the rain

Last year I was asked to train in a school that had particular issues with behaviour during wet play time. Now I don't believe in spending wet play time indoors as all of the evidence says children should be out in all weathers, but sometimes I have to work with what I get. It turned out that all the children did was watch DVD's until they became bored and misbehaved. I suggested a whole range of play activities that could take place even in a classroom. It then turned out that one of the midday staff was actually an accomplished singer in her spare time. The very next wet play time she got the children singing. It was the best wet lunchtime ever with 100% engaged children and no negative behaviour.

Make time to rhyme (yes I did!)

Rhymes represent a tiny moment of satisfaction or reward, but they also make things fundamentally easier to remember.

One fantastic use of rhyming is to teach parents of children with English as an additional language short, easy to remember rhymes that they can then share with their children. The rhyming structure allows even parents who do not speak English to be able to learn short sections in a way they could not do with straight prose. They may not know what any of the individual words actually mean but because they are easier to memorise, they can say them out loud with their children which begins to introduce English in the home and is a lovely, shared experience between parent and child, further supporting the child to become more accustomed to the new language. Basically, you don't need to know what 'grand' or 'Duke' mean, or where 'York' is to be able to learn 'The Grand Old Duke of York' and say it out loud together.

One rhyming game you can play with children is to set up rhymes for them to complete. The language can begin very simply and then become more challenging as children grow.

This is the bear that fell out of bed,

This is the bear that bumped his.........

Initially, start with just completing the final word of the rhyming line but eventually, as children grow in confidence, support them to finish more of the sentence:

This is the bear that ate all the honey.........

This is the bear.........

A dull voice does not make a dull person!

My mum was a history teacher, but she also delivered private speech and drama lessons. A man contacted her because he delivered presentations for his job and his colleagues teased him because he was very boring. He had previously been to another teacher who told him he had a naturally boring voice (he did!). My mum said that it did not matter how boring his voice was, if he sounded interested in a subject, other people were more likely to become interested. She coached him in how to sound passionate and enthusiastic, looking at facial expressions, body language and simple things like making eye contact with his audience. She then entered him into a competition for public speaking and he came second. He may not have had the vocal range of a celebrated orator (and who does?) but he was able to convey his passion and enthusiasm to an audience by clearly demonstrating his own interest.

I think this is the key. It is all too easy for adults to become jaded and cynical about the world and to let this impact on our stories, songs, and rhymes, and in fact on all of our interactions with children. It is easy to tell ourselves that we are not a good storyteller or singer or even a poet when the truth is you don't need to be a trained storyteller to tell amazing stories for your children. You don't need perfect pitch (whatever that is) to make up a song about a pooey nappy and you certainly don't need to be Shakespeare to make up rhymes. What you need is joy. If you can create happiness, stimulation and an overriding sense of safety then your children have a much greater chance at developing vital communication and language skills and, more crucially, a greater chance of thriving. I also think that if we embrace joy as a strategy when supporting children's communication and language, we might just enjoy our jobs more.

Summary

Children learn language in a different way to adults, needing not merely words but every aspect of meaning. So, joy is vitally important for giving children a complete picture of language. They learn as much about meaning through facial expressions, tone of voice, emotion, and body language as they do through the words themselves. Joy is not merely an optional extra to learning, it actually forms a foundation for creating growth mindsets and a love of learning because joyful experiences fundamentally shape the brain, making children more capable and promoting a desire to learn. The things that are most likely to be absent from children who are struggling with communication and language are songs, nursery rhymes and stories. Make stories prime time, make time to rhyme and above all sing!

4
THE JOY OF MOVEMENT AND DANCING ELEPHANTS

One of our projects is supporting newly adopted children to form bonds with their new families through shared experiences of play. We basically play out in the woods for two hours with whole families getting involved making dens, climbing trees and generally messing about.

My teenage son has begun volunteering on some of these sessions. He spent a recent session running around with one particular child, playing tag, jumping off things, giving piggy backs and just being really physically active. At the end of the session my son said to me, in a typical teenager voice, *'So is that your job? You just play?'*

What my son does not understand yet is that there is no such thing as 'just' play. To my son it was a throw away moment, but to the young boy in question it was a big deal. To have a teenager take an interest and join in physically active play is a huge deal for a young child. Especially a child that has had significant negative experiences in their life.

What my son helped that child experience was a moment of joy through physical activity and in a time where a significant proportion of children do not do enough physical activity this is hugely important. Joy is not merely a key motivator for increasing physical activity levels but for some children the *only* way to increase physical activity levels.

More, more, more!

Government guidelines on physical activity levels were recently updated. Whilst a majority of the advice remained the same, a very important sentence was added to every age category of recommended daily amounts of exercise: 'More is better' (Department of Health and Social Care, 2020).

On the subject of government guidelines, current surveys show that less than half of children are doing the recommended daily amount of exercise. In some geographical areas the figure is as low as 23 per cent (Office for Health Improvement Disparities, nd). For Early Years the figure may be even worse as one study by the National Centre for Sport and Exercise shows the figure could be as low as eight per cent (British Heart Foundation National Centre for Physical Activity and Health, 2015).

A sedentary elephant

I believe we need to address a very sedentary elephant in the room before we can even begin to understand how deeply the problem goes. So, let's be really honest here. For a significant number of people exercise sucks. I know this might seem controversial but the only reason why so many children and adults simply do not do enough exercise to be healthy is because it is an unpleasant experience. For a significant number of us, exercise can be boring, repetitive, associated with feelings of shame and humiliation, unrewarding, painful and just about the most joyless thing you can ever do. Now before I get complaints, hear me out. Every bit of research suggests that not enough people do enough exercise and whilst many reasons are cited for this the most obvious reason is that we don't enjoy it.

We need to understand this fact before we can start to come up with solutions. It is not always the case that people don't have enough time to exercise or there are not enough opportunities or even because they don't know exercise is good for us. We know exercise is good for us, we just don't enjoy it so will find excuses to avoid it. This means that for some people, no amount of information sheets or extra gym classes are going to be effective because the fundamental reason people don't do enough exercise is because it is not fun and most of us will naturally seek to avoid unpleasant experiences.

I really hope I have not offended anybody here. Sports coaches can be amazing, sport is fantastic and for those people who enjoy it, sport can be a life affirming and life-long passion. Some people love exercising and pushing their bodies to meet new challenges and goals (reward system again!). The sad truth is, a significant number of people don't feel this way.

Victory at all costs

I was the shortest child in our high school (I know this is hard to believe as people who have met me will know I am at least 6'5" now and still growing). This meant I was always the worst at almost every sport (bearing in mind that the range of sports available was severely limited in the 1980's). I will never forget doing the javelin in athletics and being so short that the javelin would drag on the ground behind me. I could only make it fly about one metre whilst everyone (including the PE teacher) laughed at my efforts. I also remember a high jump competition where I was matched against a child with a leg brace and neither of us could clear even the lowest bar. My experiences of school sport were so unrewarding that I could very easily have disengaged permanently as so many people do. I was incredibly fortunate to be able to learn badminton in sixth form and finally find a sport where my height was not a disadvantage and that I could actually enjoy. I will never be amazing and certainly have not been called up to play for my country (yet) but I still play league badminton every week and love every minute of it even when we lose (which is frequently).

Image 4.1   An elephant playing badminton by Emily

So once again we need to analyse exactly what it is that is missing from those children and adults who don't meet the required guidance for physical activity. Put simply it is joy. The simple fun of moving is absent from many people's lives because they don't conform to the very narrow view of what constitutes physical exercise. The fact that we don't enjoy running or going to the gym or Pilates does not make us wrong and it does not mean we can't experience joy in physical activity. It just means we need to find different ways to experience the joy of movement.

Who stole our joy? Part one

So, one of the reasons we don't enjoy physical exercise is that we feel like failures if we are not particularly good at something. The over emphasis on competition and success means many children (and adults) feel humiliated or uninspired. Sadly, this can start quite young, and I have experienced 3-year-olds saying that they can't do something because, to quote, *'I'm rubbish'*. This is not a natural state for a child to find themselves in. The brain/body development of a child by its very nature must incorporate a significant amount of 'failure' because this is the only way a child can develop. This means that so-called failure is not failure at all but actually an essential part of development. Take walking for instance. No child gets up and walks instantly. There are countless exploratory movements, trial and error, falling over and getting back up again, before the child can actually walk. Failure is therefore as important a process as success, in the development of this vital skill. If children gave up at the first fall, then they would never learn to walk in the first place. This means that resilience should be built-in from birth. According to the growth mindset theory by Carole Dweck (2012) this is called 'failing forward' and is a key aspect of a growth mindset. I would argue that fail forward perseverance is the natural state for a young child to be in, but that negative childhood experiences can adversely affect this. Basically, adults can undermine a child's ability to perceive failure as merely a steppingstone to success by putting too high expectations on the child. This leads to a mindset of not wanting to try because of fear of failure.

The midday supervisor of doom?

One of my roles is to train midday supervisors to support more positive play at lunchtimes. I worked with a man who was extremely overweight to the point of being obese. When he introduced himself, he said, 'the kids call me Mr Grumpy because I'm the worst member of staff in the school!' He actually seemed proud that all the children disliked him, and at lunchtime he would sit at a bench and shout at children. During our discussions around the importance of play I introduced the group to the neuroscience of play and this man started to become more and more interested in the science behind play. He became fascinated by play and began engaging fully in the training course, even to the extent of joining in all of the practical activities. Session three was all about physical activity and so we played physical playground games for over an hour. The focus of these games wasn't on winning or losing but purely on the joy of movement and this man joined in every single game because for the first time in his life nobody cared how fast or good he was. Afterwards, when he regained the ability to breathe again, he talked about his own childhood experiences of physical activity. As an overweight child, he had felt persecuted by adults for not being good enough and consequently disengaged permanently in all forms of physical activity. The very next day he went out into the playground and led the children playing the same physical games he had just learned. The most magical thing then happened. More children joined in with him than had ever joined in with the young fit sports coach that the school had specifically hired to combat obesity. At one point over forty children swarmed around this extremely overweight man, absolutely loving physical exercise, because for the first time in school history the adult couldn't catch the children in a catching game and the children could catch the adult. He didn't care about any of this, just running around with a huge grin on his face having the best lunchtime ever!

The take-away from this is that you don't have to be good at physical activity to be able to support and inspire it in your children. In fact, sometimes the best people to engage children are those who are not afraid to get it wrong some-times, who will fall over and wipe the mud from their eyes before grinning and getting right back up again.

The process focused approach

One way we can erode the joy of movement is to make it so much about winning, losing or achieving that children find the experience stressful or unrewarding. If we focus on the end product, the goal or achievement, we lose the vital motivator for physical activity. The joy in doing it in the first place.

Usain Bolt may be the world's greatest sprinter and, of course he is incredibly competitive, but he runs because he just loves running. Just by watching him you can see he gets a fierce sense of joy from pushing his body to the limits. An overwhelmingly high percentage of us are never going to be at the standard of Usain Bolt (pretty much all of us in fact). We are never going to be even remotely close to his ability level or any of the greatest athletes or sports people in the world. We are all of us different shapes, sizes and ability levels and have often grown up to feel somehow inferior because of this. I am 5'6" so even if I trained every single day, I would never be a world class sprinter because my legs are simply too short (pause for sympathy).

A tiny violin

When I was very young, I went for violin lessons. At the very first session I was told that the school did not have a violin small enough for my tiny arms and so I was sent home. My promising violin career ended right there. The tragedy is that when I tell people this, they mime playing a tiny violin in mock sympathy. Oh, the irony, if only I'd had a tiny violin back then!

So here is the problem. If we are only judging physical activity across a very narrow range of abilities, notably speed or strength, and only making those children who are good at the particular activity feel good about themselves then we are automatically failing to cater for a significant number of children. Remember, just like adults our children come in all different shapes, sizes and ability levels.

If we observe young children, we see many spontaneous and instinctive movements. We see moving at differing speeds over different surfaces, we see crawling, walking and running in all directions, we see jumping, skipping and climbing, balancing and even dancing (more on that later). All of these things existed long before humans began to group these skills into what we now know as sport. Handstands existed long before 'gymnastics' and kicking things existed long before 'football'. Children do these things because they love to push the limits of their physicality and experience joy through simple movement. Until the adult tells them they are doing it wrong.

The dog and cat world cup?

I find it interesting that many of the instinctive movements children engage in are shared with other mammals. Dogs and cats can run, jump, and even chase a ball. If we share these movements with all mammals, why do we only seem to be impressed when humans do them? We pay humans literally millions of pounds to run around a field chasing a ball. Why do we not pay Labradors? In fact, that is an FA cup final I would pay to watch, Labradors vs cats, although things might get a bit Messi! (I can only apologise for this joke.)

Image 4.2   Dogs and cats playing football

Clearly if we focus on an end product such as winning or losing, we will engage some of our children. Those children who feel like they have achieved to their own perceived level will naturally be accessing their reward system when they score a goal or win a race. A confident child might even feel good if they come second or third or if they almost achieve something. If their reward system is activated they will produce dopamine and will feel amazing. This is why some children love to compete and probably why some people become athletes in the first place. However, this approach could potentially be disengaging many of our children.

The answer is not complicated but often overlooked. Stop caring so much about winning, losing or achieving and focus on what is really important. If you can create physical experiences that are fun, stimulating, and full of joy then you can support all of our children to be physically active rather than just a few. This is an approach that I call the 'process focused approach' and it is the only way in which we can engage all of our children, even those who may already have disengaged.

The joy of water slides

One of our sessions is specifically delivered to children who are already obese or at risk of obesity. One of the favourite physical activities is the water slide which is an old bit of tarpaulin and some water and washing up liquid. Children will invariably take a long run-up to slide down the water slide usually accompanied by huge grins and much laughter. What these children are actually doing is sprinting. Their levels of physical activity throughout the session are incredibly high and yet despite being red-faced and out of breath, at no point do the children realise they are 'exercising' in the conventional sense. There is no way that any of these children would 'sprint' as part of a sports session, but they happily run at full speed to make the water slide even more fun.

This is the point I am trying to make. There is simply no way you could make these children run through any other means because they have already had such negative experiences of physical activity. They will actively avoid any attempt to get them moving on an adult's terms because this has previously caused them pain and even humiliation. Only by focusing on the joy of movement through the simple act of sliding down a water slide can we unlock the child's desire to be physically active. For some children then, the process focused approach is not merely a good way to engage them but the only way.

The process focused approach is also vitally important for inclusion. Because it focuses not on any level of achievement but on the joy of the experience then we can accommodate children with the broadest range of needs. If there is no perceived level of competence for children to compare themselves to then there can be no stigma of failure and children can access an activity at whatever level they feel confident without fear of humiliation.

Never give up, never surrender!

One dad on our adopted children's sessions decided to pull his son on the scooter boards. Another child joined in and then another and because the scooter boards connect to each other, he ended up with a chain of scooter boards with about twelve children sitting expectantly. Pulling twelve children on scooter boards on a smooth surface may not pose too much of a problem but these children were on grass. Red in the face and breathing heavily he pulled every single child whilst the scooter boards dug a deep groove in the grass. Even though it nearly killed him, there was no way he was giving up because he was determined to be the best dad he could be for his children!

Competition is not always bad for children but…

When I deliver training to sports coaches they sometimes struggle with this approach because they initially think it means that we avoid all competition which would ultimately prevent children from being competitive and excelling.

This is NOT the case. Competition is not intrinsically bad for children and is in fact a natural part of play. The problem only arises when adults handle the concept of competition so badly that they disengage more children than they engage.

A classic example is when a sports coach plays a game with children where if you lose or do not do well at the game then you are now 'out' of the game. A child now must stand and watch whilst other children have fun playing and this is somehow meant to make the child better at the game or make them try harder when they are allowed back into the game. Even a cursory look at this strategy shows how utterly flawed it is when working with children. The sole purpose of a sports coach is to support children to engage and improve at a sport. This is the one thing that absolutely cannot happen if the child is excluded from playing the very sport they are trying to improve at. Put simply, a child cannot improve at a sport (or any physical activity) through telepathy; they actually have to play it to improve (or, it turns out, imagining themselves playing will help them improve too - see Chapter 2!).

I think the issue is that there is a mistaken belief that giving children negative experiences inspires them to try harder and helps them to be able to cope better with negative experiences in the future. This is not true. I can say with absolute certainty, after working with vulnerable children for over thirty years, that negative experiences do not make children 'tougher', they do not make children try harder and they certainly do not support children to excel.

There might be some children who are confident enough of their own abilities that the occasional negative experience might inspire them to try harder, but these are the minority. Confident children can sometimes push themselves outside their comfort zone to achieve and can thrive in higher stress situations. However, this can only happen if the stress is within certain limits and only if the child has a fundamental belief in themselves. So, competition can be healthy for some children but constantly feeling rubbish about your abilities does not inspire physical activity but undermines it. So yes, it is OK to be competitive, but this should never be a child's only experience of physical activity and it should not be at the expense of less confident children. It is fine to have a winner but if we focus too much on the winning, we forget how important the joy of movement is. The process focused approach does not preclude competitive play but shifts the emphasis from the winning or achieving to enjoying and engaging. The ideal situation is that even if we are being competitive, we are enjoying the experience so much that win or lose we will still try our hardest and will not disengage if we lose.

Our own experiences impact on children

Another way in which we prevent children experiencing joy in physical activity is through our own attitudes as adults. Bearing in mind that a majority of adults do not do enough physical activity because they do not enjoy it, then the realistic role models for physical activity are simply not there. Also bear in mind that for some children as they get older the role models for physical activity become more and more unattainable. The footballers and athletes in the media are all at the peak of human fitness and ability, something that most of us can't even come close to. As children begin to make the inevitable comparisons to themselves and the adults around them, they can become more likely to compare themselves negatively with the pinnacles of sport that we see all the time. This is because often the only adults they see being physically active are the ones who have the kind of physique that most of us will never have. Additionally, if children's existing role models actively detest physical activity and portray body language equating physical activity with discomfort, pain, or inconvenience then we are already starting children on the road to reluctance.

A comedy groan

I watched my son, when he was 3-years-old, pick up a toy and make a strange groaning sound. I turned around to see my wife laughing. 'He's doing you!' she said. I have two bad knees and for the last few years have been making a groaning sound whenever I bend over. My son was simply emulating this behaviour.

So, the antidote to this is the adult who regardless of ability, body shape, size, or even age shows children it is OK to be active. The overweight midday supervisor inspired children to move more because even the most underconfident of children were thinking, '*If he can do it, I can do it!*' Children absolutely need to see more role models who are not the young fit sports coaches or runners or cyclists. In short, they need to see us, the ordinary people showing children that not only is it OK to move but it can be really fun.

What does this look like in practice?

First and foremost, we need to acknowledge that children will all have different abilities, and we should never expect them to be the same when it comes to physical activity. We need to understand that some children can jump off one step and some can jump off five steps and this in no way makes one child better than another. We need to stop assigning value to some movements and less to others, accepting that some children will find joy from running and jumping, kicking a ball and even competing but many more children will find joy in dancing, pretending to be a worm, standing on one leg and spinning around until they feel sick. These attributes may not officially be recognised as sports but are just as important and worthwhile as any other physical movement. I do think it might help if the Olympic committee recognised 'pretending you are a worm' and 'spinning around until you feel sick' as official new events for the 2024 Olympics in Tokyo to inspire a new generation of champions and I'm sure you can all think of a child who would excel at these events.

Secondly, we need to throw out ideas of only focusing on winning or achieving and make physical activity what it should be about, joy. We need to focus on the process of moving rather than any end product that might arise. We need to remember that getting it wrong is merely a steppingstone and a natural one at that.

Early years readers already know that joy is intrinsically important to physical activity and would never dream of doing an activity which excludes children if they lose, right? Except, I realised recently that I have been playing a game with young children for years which does exactly what I have been warning everyone of. Musical statues!

Musical statues is evil?

If you think about it objectively, musical statues is an evil game made up by evil adults. Firstly, it penalises movement and secondly, it excludes the child who moves, forcing them to watch other children have fun whilst they stand still, and if they were any good at standing still, they wouldn't be out in the first place! So recently I have adapted musical statues to fit in with my beliefs about joy. There are several versions of the game that we use. The simplest version is, 'Follow the Leader Musical Statues'. For this version you assign one child to be the leader and then turn on the music and the children all dance. The difference comes when the music stops because instead of a child being 'out', every child (and adult) has to 'freeze' in the same pose as the child who is the leader. A new leader is then assigned until every child has had a go. So, you now have all the benefits of musical statues, the dancing, the rhythmic movements and the trying to be still but no child feels excluded and the movement is for everyone. In addition, the child who is the leader feels important and empowered. Yes, there will be some children who deliberately do the splits to catch out the adults playing but this is part of the fun, and no judgement is ever made if children do not duplicate the leader's 'pose' accurately.

The power of dance

This segways nicely into dancing as one of the key ways in which we inspire movement in our children. There is something unbelievably powerful about music as a motivator for movement and also something uniquely human about our ability to dance. Once again, we are far beyond the realm of animals here. Animals might sometimes appear to dance (see all of YouTube!) and there is some suggestion that particularly musically inclined parrots can keep to a beat 25 per cent of the time (Krulwich, 2014). However, no other animal takes dancing to the same level as humans, reliably moving in intricate ways to a huge variety of beats and melodies from hip hop to bhangra.

How is this linked to joy? Well, there appears to be a unique form of happiness that comes when we move to a beat. Of course, it can't just be a beat by itself, we need all of the other bits of music that make it interesting. It could be that the rules music follows mean that just like rhyming there is a sense of completion and maybe a tiny hit of dopamine when a particular tune or beat appeals to us. It could also be that instinctively moving to a beat bypasses some of the reluctance to move that we may have had instilled from our childhood, allowing us to experience the endorphins that we may no longer experience from more structured physical exercise. (Hence the incredibly sweaty mess I become at a wedding.) Whatever the reason, dancing gives us joy. It is highly likely then, that when moving to a beat we not only produce endorphins but, if we dance with somebody else, the shared moment of joy will also be producing oxytocin and supporting social bonding. The rhythmic movements will also be activating our reward system producing dopamine.

We also need to consider the fact that early childhood movement is incredibly important for brain growth and is in fact an essential process underpinning all other development. Whilst all movement is good for children, spontaneous dancing gives a hugely broad range of movements making it neurologically and developmentally extremely rich. For children, dancing is innately process-focused with almost no consideration of a goal or end product, just the joy of being in the moment.

Not just for children

Just in case you thought dancing was just good for young children, there are several studies showing the benefits of dancing for elderly people. Dance can increase memory and promote brain health and could potentially alleviate symptoms of dementia and other age-related diseases.

Whatever the reason, there is something truly magical about a group of young children dancing with joy. There is clearly something about certain tunes and beats, and it is different for all of us, that make us experience joy to such an extent that we cannot help but physically respond. When you add to this that music has the power to calm us down and reduce anxiety then it becomes an essential tool for creating magical experiences for our children.

The children's mix tape

One lovely idea is when you find out information about a child when they start at your setting, make sure to ask what their favourite music is. You can then make a 'mix tape' of your children's favourite tunes to dance to. Not only will this inspire children to dance, but it can also help make them feel emotionally secure and make your setting a home from home. It will also potentially introduce children to different types of music from a broad range of genres and cultures that they may not experience in the home. One minute you are Bollywood dancing, the next head-banging to heavy metal!

Funky cave people

If music predated speech, then it stands to reason that dance also evolved very early in the development of humans. Was this the first kind of movement that was purely for its own sake? The first kind of movement that wasn't motivated solely by instinct or for a purpose such as hunting or survival? This makes self-expression through dance one of the earliest art forms and hugely significant for our species and means that when our children dance, they are upholding a tradition from potentially 200,000 years ago.

Image 4.3 Cave people dancing

Adults showing joy

So, whatever our body shape, fitness level, age or technical ability we need to be showing joy in a variety of movements to inspire our children to experience the same joy. We need to be dancing, jumping, running and twirling, even if (like me) we cannot do any of those things successfully. Honestly, if I spin round just once at my age I feel nauseous for half an hour afterwards! We can't follow the line of thinking that says movement is for other people, because if we do then our children may come to the same conclusion. There is nothing wrong with having a specialist dance company attending your setting to do dancing with the children but please make sure that is not the only time children dance. Don't just blow bubbles for children to chase but chase them yourself! Show our children that movement is joyful for everyone, not just the minority who are good at it.

I'll be there for you...

Some of you may remember an episode of *Friends* where Phoebe runs in an unusual, albeit joyful way. She flails her arms around and looks so silly that Rachel is initially embarrassed to be with her. She then realises that running is much more fun if you flail your arms about. Maybe we all need to be a bit more like Phoebe and care less about what we look like when we move and more about the joy it can bring.

Movement built in

We need to make joyful movement an integral part of the day. Everything from transitioning between indoors and outdoors to getting ready for lunch can be full of joyful movements.

Why not have a jumping door. Every time a child or adult crosses the threshold, they do a little jump. It does not matter how high just so long as the children have fun jumping. Mix it up by jumping whilst pulling a funny face or add a challenge because today it's a hopping door. It doesn't even need to be a door, just a line on the ground.

Another weird idea is to mess with gravity. You probably don't have a rock face for climbing in your setting or home. You all have a floor though, so with a little imagination you can pretend the floor is the cliff face and you can pretend to climb up it with all the accompanying grunts and straining. This is a completely different sort of movement to moving across the floor in a conventional way.

On the subject of grunts and straining, a lovely (and silly) activity is to create a weightlifting weight with a stick and two balloons. Now obviously the balloons don't weigh much so lifting the 'weight' is simple. However, you encourage the children to pretend the weight is really heavy and act accordingly. This encourages a completely different set of movements and an increased level of control whilst pretending the weight is heavy. This is not just a joyful physical movement but manipulating objects, using imagination and a healthy dose of self-expression. One word of caution, one of my staff team 'fake strained' so hard that she broke wind loudly in front of the children who naturally thought this was hilarious.

Mirroring is really powerful for children and simple copying activities are really rich. This makes 'follow the leader' a really important game which can create so many different types of movement. Just make sure it is not always the adult who is the leader as being the leader can be a wonderful empowering experience for our children.

One type of play that is declining is the rhyming and singing games that we used to play in school or nursery. Games such as 'Here we go round the mulberry bush', 'Ring a ring o' roses' and 'In and out the dusty bluebells'. I regularly see children absolutely delighted by these rhyming games.

How about making a car out of a cardboard box and the child's legs stick out the bottom? They will run at top speed just to make the car go faster and won't even realise they are sprinting. We also did the same thing but made aeroplanes. Their movements became completely different as the children swooped, turned and jumped whilst experiencing the joy of 'flying'.

A water fight with a sinister twist

Water balloons are pretty rubbish. If you want a decent water fight you can forget it. The balloons don't seem to pop when they hit someone, only when they subsequently hit the ground. And oh my goodness the amount of time and effort it takes to fill the things! So, we use sponge balls or simply sponges instead. A paddling pool full of sponge balls creates a ready made and instant cache of ammunition and you get much wetter (which is after all the point of a water fight). On one of our sessions, it became so hot that after the water fight a number of social workers and foster carers decided to bathe their feet in the paddling pool to cool off. Unfortunately, after lunch another water fight ensued whereby all of the children decided to throw sponge balls at me. Sponge balls that had now been soaked in manky foot water. (Ugh!) Did I mention I don't like feet!

Spontaneous movements

Just as music inspires movement there are certain other activities which mean children can't help but move. We do a lovely activity called wind angels where we simply tie (or tape) multiple streamers to children's arms. They cannot help but flap their arms to experience the sensation of the streamers billowing. They soon work out that the faster they move the more the streamers will billow and soon are flapping and swooping, usually without an adult needing to tell them how to move. If your children appear hesitant at first, make sure that one of the adults is also a wind angel running and swooping with joy.

Note

If you have a significant birthday, you may have had one of the birthday banners with your age on it. These are made from a kind of light-weight metallic plastic foil and are absolutely fantastic for making streamers from. They are really cheap to buy, and one birthday banner will make lots of streamers. Not only do they shimmer in the sun they make a wonderful rustling noise when children wave their arms. You can also use these shiny streamers to wrap around hoops to make them rustle or even attach to balls for throwing.

Another thing that weirdly inspires movement is magic potions. Basically, children make the magic potion (using anything from food colouring and glitter to mud and shells) and then shake it. Now if you hand an adult a bottle that needs shaking, they will naturally shake it using their hands and arms. Not so with young children. For some reason many children will shake the potion using their whole bodies with almost every bit of them involved in the shaking process. These kinds of whole-body movements are really developmentally rich and have the added benefit of being genuinely funny to watch, although make sure the lid is on tight.

A 3-year-old is unlikely to be able to hit a moving tennis ball with a tennis bat. They may have seen people on TV do it or even their parents, but it is probably beyond the ability of most very young children. Why not hang a ball on a string from a washing line or climbing frame? The child can happily hit the ball and watch it fly.

If we make movement a natural part of our day with more spontaneous movement, more dancing and more silliness then we should easily reach and exceed the current government guidance on activity levels. Then we are not scrambling to come up with activities to support children to reach their recommended daily amount of physical activity because we have already exceeded them with all of the wonderful movements children do as part of their day. Remember 'More is better!'

Different types of movement

You don't consider a child to have mastered walking if they can only walk in straight lines and on flat surfaces. Children need to be able to walk backwards, forwards and sideways on flat ground, slopes, sticky surfaces or slippery surfaces. They need to be able to walk with or without shoes on grass or on carpet or wood. Sometimes our early years environments can be limiting because everything is flat and safe. Where possible we need to make sure our environment can change and adapt as children grow.

In baby rooms one very simple way to support babies to move on a variety of different surfaces and slopes is to let babies crawl all over you. The human body is a very varied surface and baby room workers can massively enhance tummy time and early movement by being a wonderful adaptable resource. One day you are a bouncy castle for your children, the next a ski slope and the next a rugged terrain.

A tummy time extravaganza

On the subject of tummy time, I cannot stress just how important this is for children. We are looking at those early movements being fundamentally important for every aspect of a baby's development and brain growth. We actually deliver tummy time training and one thing we are sometimes hearing from parents is that their babies don't like tummy time, so they stop doing it. One reason babies don't like tummy time is because they are being placed in an unfamiliar environment that feels, smells and looks different and they are now considerably further away from their carer. One simple answer to this is that the carer or key worker needs to be lying on the floor too, face to face with their baby showing them that this is a safe place, and that tummy time is fun. In short, even our youngest babies react if we show joy in physical movements.

Note for out of school settings

It is worth noting that many of the activities I have just described work equally well with older children. The wind angels activity is also loved by our 7-year-olds and even our teenagers have played the pretend weight lifting game. The one thing that is really important for the out of school setting is the process focused approach. Almost the entirety of children's experiences of primary school are goal focused, from the PE lessons to the spelling test. This is exhausting for some children and the constant pressure of a goal focused day

can mean some children really struggle, especially with behaviour. It is absolutely vital that the out of school setting does not just give children more of
the same experiences they have had all day. Remember, play is a process and a
good playworker focuses on children enjoying the moment of play rather than
on the end product. For the out of school club, physical activity should always
be about joy and fun rather than winning or losing. There should be healthy
amounts of silliness with no child ever made to feel like a failure for not being
able to do something because they may have had enough of that in their school
day. Children encounter lots of serious adults so what they need most in out of
school settings are fun adults. The other thing that out of school settings need
to be mindful of is that children may have had a very sedentary day at school.
They absolutely need to move and what many of them need is boisterous and
highly physical play. In short, Hama beads and colouring just won't cut it for
some children. We must make sure that children get as many opportunities for
joyful physical movements as possible, otherwise we are almost guaranteeing
negative behaviour.

Budding Robin Hoods

I trained coaches from an archery club in the process focused approach as it is one
of the cornerstones of inclusive practice and engages children with a broad range
of abilities and support needs. They instantly revised their entire approach to
teaching archery to make it more about the joy of the sport rather than teaching
specific skills. One simple change they made was to shoot water balloons rather
than archery targets. They said the children loved the new approach and became
much more engaged, which consequently made them more proficient.

I see you ninja!

Even a simple game of tag can be anxiety making for some children. Bear in
mind that tag really only favours fast children, so it is not always enjoyed by
slower children. I vividly remember being the smallest child and struggling to
catch the jeering bigger children. So instead of just perpetuating the same old
feelings of insecurity and humiliation, change things up to make it much more
about joy. One version of tag we play is called Last Ninja. You can download
how to play it from my website (www.iinspired.org.uk). This is my go-to physical
game for out of school club although we also play it with our younger children.
Basically, instead of one child being on and then passing on the tag to subsequently slower children, the initial person who is on (the Chief Ninja) stays
on for the whole game and every subsequent person they catch joins them in
being on until eventually everyone is caught. The beauty of this version is that

with the exception of the first child, no child is singled out. We have played this game with over 200 children ranging from 5- to 15-years-old. Groups of roving 5-year-olds would gang up together to take down a 15-year-old and the whole experience is way more inclusive than a normal game of tag.

Stop winning – just stop

I glanced out of a school window recently and saw a football coach running towards the goal during a football match. His skill was genuinely impressive as he beat one defender, then another and finally, one on one with the goalie, scored a goal before running around the field celebrating. What was slightly less impressive was that this was reception class. If you find yourself needing validation by crushing 5-year-olds, then re-think.

I also think we have a unique opportunity to show children a different sort of role model. Remember even very young children may have grown up watching footballers take dives and effectively 'cheat' to try to win a game. They will have seen fights on pitch, arguments with referees and an attitude of win at all costs, and 'it only counts as cheating if you get caught'. If as an adult we find ourselves playing a physical game with children, let's show them an alternative role model. Give children the benefit of the doubt. Show them how to play fairly and considerately and they may just enjoy the game more. They will certainly find it less stressful.

Play is a big deal

Remember at the beginning of this chapter I talked about my son running around with an adopted child. What my son didn't know is that when this child had first been adopted, he was obese and at severe risk of health problems. Prior to adoption he had barely been allowed to move at all and was kept strapped into his pushchair and fed on junk food. Fast forward to the present day and this child is with the most wonderful nurturing family and absolutely loves physical movement of all kinds. So, my son was not just sharing play with this child but was giving him the one type of play he had had restricted in his earliest years. Like I said to my son, there is no such thing as just play, play is always a big deal for children.

I occasionally encounter adults who when playing a game with children will deliberately and obviously cheat in an attempt to be amusing. It is part of the culture of banter that we will be addressing in a later chapter. Children do not find this funny or clever. If anything, they find this behaviour confusing and not a little annoying. Let's be better than this. Remember that many children will not understand the messages that this behaviour gives them. Realistically they get enough examples of negative adults in the media, so why don't we show them something different. How can we expect children to play fairly if adults don't show them how.

Change the rules

Do what works with your children. Last Ninja may work really well with your children but if they struggle or are too young then play Crocodile, Crocodile (also on my website) instead. Never feel like you are constrained by the rules though. If my version of Crocodile, Crocodile doesn't work for your children then change the rules so that it does. Instead of one crocodile to start, have twenty. Make them robots instead of crocodiles. In short do everything you can so that children can enjoy physical activity. If the rules of a game or activity are getting in the way of the joy of moving, then change them or throw them out entirely. Remember that for the older generation like me, some of the best games were ones we just made up on the spur of the moment.

Interestingly one of the other animals that can move to a beat is elephants. Maybe the elephant in the room wasn't so sedentary after all, maybe he was tapping his foot to a hip hop beat?

The return of badminton

So, it turns out I am not the only person who enjoys badminton despite struggling at all other sports. One of our adopted children played badminton recently and his parents said it was the first time he had ever enjoyed a sport. Whilst the parents were telling me this, another set of parents overheard and said, 'Well we actually met playing badminton!' The adoption agency representative chimed in with, 'I play badminton with my family.' To which I replied, 'I play badminton too!' So, we have now decided to take the families to play badminton together. We have subsequently been successful in a funding bid for a badminton project for adopted children!

Summary

So, we learnt that joy is not merely important for physical activity but it's key motivator and if we remove that joy, we ultimately disengage children. A significant number of children disengage in physical activity and a huge percentage of adults simply don't do enough exercise. The answer to this crisis is emphatically joy. Joy is the only way we can re-engage children who have already disengaged. The way we use this joy is through the process focused approach which focuses not on any goal or end product but firmly on the process of enjoying the experience. This removes failure thresholds and supports children with a broad range of abilities and additional needs to participate without fear of humiliation. The best way we can encourage our children to move more is by showing them positive role models and by sharing our own joyful movements. Most importantly you don't need to be a young fit sports coach to inspire movement. People come in all shapes and sizes and physical activity is for all of us. We also discussed the fact that physical activity is not all about sport, and in fact many of the wonderful childhood movements existed long before we began to call them sport. You may find no joy in running or going to the gym, I know I certainly don't, but we can still find joy in dancing, pretending we are a worm and silliness. We learnt once again that play is a big deal and there is no such thing as *just* play. If only someone would write a book about play? We also learnt that dancing is the most amazing thing, and that music inspires unique joyful movements. Oh, and parrots and elephants can dance.

Image 4.4 A dancing elephant by L

5

THE JOY OF POO AND
A SCHOOL FOR NINJAS

One thing that is becoming clear to me whilst writing this book is that we seem to be prioritising the wrong things in society. There is one aspect of development in particular that is never once mentioned in any curriculum documents or on the EYFS but will be used by a majority of people far more than they ever use maths, geography or any number of academic skills. I am of course talking about humour.

Now, I am not trying to downplay the importance of maths in society, after all it is an integral part of almost every advancement humans have ever made. However, the fact that humour is not recognised as a vital social function is a glaring omission in the holistic development of our children.

Humour is massively important in our society. Sense of humour is frequently cited as a highly desirable social trait in friends or partners and the comedy industry is extremely lucrative with some comedians earning millions. Humour is something that many of us will experience almost every day, whether it is a shared joke with a colleague or a funny video on YouTube. Sit coms, panel-shows and stand-up are so ingrained in modern life that it would be difficult to imagine a world without comedy and humour. Humour is an integral aspect of our social skills and a vital form of social interaction. Humour can diffuse a stressful situation and help us deal with tragedy. Humour brings joy to millions of people and is a fundamental part of what it means to be human in the first place.

Clearly then, a sense of humour is a vital developmental process. In our duty to prepare our children for adulthood the concept of humour would seem to be extremely important and something that should be embedded into good practice. And yet, just like joy, humour seems to be completely absent.

This seems to be a rather large omission. I would argue that we are missing something really important, and we need to address this if we are going to give our children the joyful experience so essential for their life-long well-being.

It is worth bearing in mind that the level of divergent thinking, creative problem-solving and imagination required to say something genuinely funny is extremely high. If other people find it funny too then the level of social awareness is also extremely high. Funny children can be some of the most intelligent children we ever work with and yet this is not always recognised and often even discouraged. In terms of brain growth, the spontaneous creativity of a joke or witty remark is incredibly neurologically rich which means children encouraged and supported to be funny could be physically growing their brains.

Unrepeatable

As a child the funniest thing I ever said in class was a joke in an English lesson which unfortunately I can't print. Believe me when I say it was genuinely hilarious and involved the word 'symbolics'. Naturally I got sent to the head teacher for my efforts.

Another issue is that, just like any developmental process, humour has to start somewhere. This means that for our youngest children, who are just starting this process, humour can be, well let's just say, very basic. Being realistic we are not going to get complex wordplay from children who are still developing their vocabulary. We are not going to get insightful observational comedy from children whose life experiences have been limited, and we are certainly unlikely to get biting political satire from a 3-year-old.

A 3-year-old's political joke

Question: What is the Prime Minister's economic policy?
Answer: Bogey!
(Note - This is actually true.)

So, you begin to see the problem. Children's early sense of humour tends to consist of poo, farts, and bogeys. Exactly the concepts that some adults will find rude or undesirable. I have had parents complain when I read the wonderful book, *The Dinosaur that Pooped a Planet!* because they considered it inappropriate. There is even a review of this book on Amazon which says, *'Do not buy this book, it is about poo'*.

Thirty children shouting POO!

The Dinosaur that Pooped a Planet! is an awesome book. Its rhyme scheme is incredibly well-crafted, and it is a unique and engaging story. It is also genuinely funny to young children. If you can get all of your children to join in with the page that says 'POO' in huge letters, then they are fully engaged in the story. You are showing them that stories are fun, funny, mischievous and above all full of joy. Remember, if children experience joy in stories, they might just want to write their own stories.

The trouble is that if we restrict these early explorations of humour we are potentially impacting on the child's progression into more advanced humour. Also, if we're being honest, some of you giggled at the word 'poo' and you are adults. I think therefore that we can be overly strict with children's humour. We need to recognise its limitations and celebrate children's humour. Far from being inappropriate, this is the start of something very special.

Comedy lessons

The excellent poet and performer Rob Gee delivers comedy workshops for children in schools. One thing he frequently notes is the profound impact of these sessions especially for children who struggle to engage in more formal learning. The imagination and creativity he inspires, with children who don't always show this through other aspects of learning, is truly heart-warming. He has also written a poem about an evil magician so is clearly a man of intelligence and insight!

Laughter is awesome

Another thing we do if we restrict humour is to restrict its outcome, laughter. Laughter is an instantly recognisable outpouring of joy and is hugely beneficial. Every bit of advice in terms of adult mental health says we need to laugh more, not less. Its benefit to children though is incalculable.

A recent study shows that social laughter, shared with other humans, increases the amount of opioids in our brain (Manninen et al., 2017). Opioids are chemicals with a similar effect to morphine! This means that we get high on shared laughter.

Other studies show increased endorphin levels in the brain when we laugh (Berk et al., 1989). Remember endorphins are essential feel-good chemicals that are intrinsically important for emotional well-being and mental health. This means laughter is vitally important for our children and a key component of their well-being.

There are even studies that show laughter can help us cope with pain! This means the more we laugh, the more physically resilient we become, with one study showing that we are able to cope with 15 per cent more pain if we have laughed before experiencing pain (Dunbar et al., 2011).

This is hugely significant for childcare settings because if we can make our children laugh, when they do inevitably fall over, they are now more likely to shrug off the pain and carry on playing rather than immediately needing an adult to help them. This could be really helpful for outdoor and risky play because it makes children fundamentally more resilient and better able to cope with life! Laughter is better than any cold compress!

What fascinates me is how they investigated this odd fact. Basically, the scientists used various devices (a frozen wine cooler being one) to inflict pain on their subjects (or victims). Subjects were then asked to express when they could no longer tolerate the pain. When the subjects had laughed before the experiments, they could withstand 15 per cent more pain. Am I a bad person for thinking this sounds hilarious? I can just imagine a group of scientists sitting around chatting saying, *'What shall we do for today's experiments?'* and one of them says, *'Hey, let's cause lots of people pain!'* and the whole group descends into maniacal laughter (which ironically makes them more able to cope with pain!).

Another study shows that laughter reduces the levels of stress hormones such as cortisol. We will see in a subsequent chapter just how profoundly important this is for our children. However, even the anticipation of laughter reduces stress hormones (American Physiological Society, 2008). This means that as your children walk towards your setting already anticipating the laughter and joy they will undoubtedly experience in your care, they automatically reduce the level of toxic stress hormones and arrive at your setting in the optimum biochemical state for well-being, learning and development and joy.

It gets better: there are claims that laughter can improve our immune system and increase blood flow which helps prevent heart attacks and other cardiovascular issues. It can even help us to live longer (Robinson, 2018).

So, laughter is clearly a vital aspect of our social behaviour and well-being, intrinsically important for mental health and a fundamental social process shared with all humans. Once again it is not mentioned on the EYFS or Development Matters or National Curriculum. Surely this is wrong? If we have clear research showing us the immense value of laughter in our lives why is this not a fundamental aspect of all education?

All of this means that if your children's setting is a place full of laughter your children will flood with all of the positive biochemicals associated with joy and even their anticipation of arriving at the setting will lower their stress levels. They will then feel better, learn better and even cope with pain better. This will also do the same for the adults!

Education is a funny business

I said we are more likely to use humour in our lives than maths or geography but what if the maths or geography teacher makes the lesson funny? Well, the old adage, *'If you are laughing you are learning'* is particularly true here. We all remember the teachers who made the effort to be funny, to make jokes and make the subject entertaining. I would bet it is not just the teacher you remember, though. You probably remember more of what was taught.

This is where laughter becomes really important for learning. If a child laughs whilst learning they will flood with positive biochemicals, some of which are addictive, like opioids. Remember, the anticipation of laughter produces the same chemicals, so if a learning experience is funny then children will crave that learning experience. They will also retain much more of the information taught.

This has been really important for my career. In my early days as an inexperienced trainer, I wanted to get across to my learners the real-life, everyday experiences of working with children. It never occurred to me to try and make it funny. Over the years of developing my training I found that certain real-life stories about children would get people laughing and when they did, they would instantly become more engaged in the training. I came to realise that laughter was an incredibly potent tool, not just for working with children but for training adults. Now many years later I carefully craft sections of learning to make sure there are moments of laughter. The jokes and funny stories are a deliberate way to enhance the training because from experience it is by far the most effective way to get through to people. Even hostile groups will come round to your way of thinking if you can make them laugh. Now obviously my jokes don't always work, after all I am a play specialist not a comedian, but I try to use comedy to get across some really important messages.

So, the terrible jokes in this book notwithstanding, humour is clearly vitally important as a tool for teaching and learning. Think of our secondary education system if every teacher had mandatory stand-up comedy lessons!

Bob Hughes was a play theorist who was incredibly significant in the field of playwork and a genuine legend of play. He famously proposed 16 distinct types of play in his *Taxonomy of Play Types* (Hughes, 2002). He cites 'jokes' as a key example of communication play.

What's in a joke?

One aspect of a joke that makes it funny is the unexpected nature of the punchline. The surprise or incongruity of the ending is what makes it funny. This also ties in with our understanding of the reward system. The completion of the joke activates the reward system producing dopamine, but the dopamine is increased because the happiness is surprising. This has also been noted in babies' laughter responses. Babies laugh more at spontaneous, unpredictable stimuli than at experiences that are repeated or expected. The simple joy of peek-a-boo will wane if repeated in the same way, but the laughter remains fresh if different faces are pulled or different tones of voice used (George Scarlett et al., 2005).

Children often seek this incongruity in their own early explorations of humour. My son, when he was around 2-years-old spent quite some time trying to balance a potato on the cat's head and then laughing when it fell off. Children will create incongruity by wearing their pants on their head or sticking their foot in the custard. This is not negative behaviour but a means to explore humour.

Image 5.1   Loitering with intent to put a potato on a cat's head

Smell of onions?

One of my son's favourite puppets was a Welsh dragon called Idris. Idris would sniff people and then tell them what they smelled of. He would sidle up to someone, sniff them and then declare, 'Smells of salami?' Or 'Onion' or the biggest laugh of all, 'Smells of poo'. The build up to the word 'poo' would add to the anticipation and the incongruity of people smelling of unusual things caused my son to laugh out loud time and time again.

Far from being trivial these early explorations of humour are vitally important for the development of social abilities. In fact, the eminent psychologist Lev Vygotsky believed that humorous social interactions actually facilitate a child's cognitive development (Vygotsky, 1978).

What about mischief?

So where does that leave mischief? Blurring the lines between positive and negative behaviour is a strange kind of behaviour that clearly gives joy but can also be interpreted as negative. Think of the children you work with. There are some that just seem to have this air of mischief that make them both challenging and fascinating at the same time. The children I remember the most are the ones who had that twinkle in their eyes and you couldn't leave them alone with felt tip pens.

The unvarnished truth

A 5-year-old girl once looked at me quizzically and then announced, 'Your eyebrows do my head in!' Ouch!

There is also a kind of adult who views this mischief as a deliberate afront and takes it very personally. It then becomes a battle of wills between an increasingly angry adult and an increasingly frustrated child until the adult usually emotionally overpowers the child with anger and hostility to curb the mischievous behaviour.

I think if you look at some of the world's greatest thinkers you will often see mischief. If you ever see the legendary mathematician Stephen Hawkins in an interview, you will see that despite all the challenges he faced he still had that sense of mischief. I think therefore, there are links between mischievousness and divergent thinking, and I believe mischief is linked to creative problem solving. Mischief can involve finding loopholes, creatively pushing the boundaries of behaviour, and even coming up with clever ideas. These are exactly the traits you would associate with a creative problem solver.

So, I don't have a problem with mischievous children. I don't feel the need to crush the mischief out of them in the pursuit of perfect behaviour. I actually think if you can support that child to understand just how amazing they are you could actually help foster a trait that could one day change the world. I even include elements of mischief in my work with children (more on that later).

In my previous book I touched upon this study briefly. J. Nina Leiberman was looking at the traits in early childhood that potentially lead to a mindset of creative problem solving or divergent thinking (Edwards and Lieberman, 2014). She cites 'sense of humour' as a key element in the development of a creative mindset. So, here we have a simple study suggesting that humour is incredibly rich in developing creative problem solving which is one of the most important life skills. This means that sense of humour is not just important for an individual but for our society as a whole. With the current problems facing humanity we need as many creative thinkers as possible. We also need a laugh to get us through the dark times.

Another key aspect of humour is its impact on our mental health. Rob Gee, who I mentioned earlier, also does comedy workshops with adults who have mental health conditions. What is interesting is that many of the adults make jokes about their illness or about mental health in general as a way of coping and expressing themselves.

Two very naughty boys!

There is a wonderful documentary on the BBC with the Dalai Lama and Archbishop Desmond Tutu discussing the concept of joy (BBC Four, 2022). What is immediately obvious is the mischief and humour with which they both view the world. At one point the interviewer asks these very old men what they think about death and both men instantly burst out laughing.

There is clearly something incredibly cathartic about humour, even in the darkest of times, and this perhaps illustrates humour at its most powerful, as a fundamental coping mechanism for life. Our ability to laugh together, even when times are at their toughest, is a uniquely human trait and a precious gift we can give to our children. We therefore need to recognise humour, not merely as something frivolous but as a vital social function, profoundly important for our children's well-being.

What does this look like in practice?

We need to foster a culture of laughter in our practice. Rather than dismissing this simple human reaction as an optional extra to childhood we need to acknowledge just how vital a childhood full of laughter can be. If adults are laughing, then the children are more likely to laugh too. If adults are not merely acknowledging the child's sense of humour but actively encouraging and joining in with humour, then the child feels important and worthwhile but is also more likely to laugh.

Remember that not all children have the same sense of humour, so we need to try and find what makes each of our children laugh. It might be a story about poo, it might be a funny face or a tickle or a funny noise. It might even be a joke or play on words. One of the key components of early humour is a sense of incongruity so sometimes just doing something unusual and surprising will cause children to laugh. If it is both funny and surprising, then it will increase dopamine production.

Laughter brings the brain under control. By this I mean that it is a key mechanism for calming down the amygdala (the fear and anger centre of our brain). Children will actually begin to synchronise their mood, emotions and behaviour with the adults in their vicinity. This means that if we are struggling emotionally then our children could also be struggling. Laughter is a key mechanism for getting our brain back under control, so if ever we feel like we are stressed or anxious we can use laughter as a quick fix to alleviate stress, which will ultimately help our children to experience less stress. With this in mind

Image 5.2   A cat running into a window by K

there should be lots of opportunities for humour in a setting. Managers can put funny pictures up in the staff room or on the back of the toilet doors. You can bring jokes in for your colleagues or just tell funny stories. Let's be honest, the children do many funny things during our time with them and sometimes just relating what Sunam did with the box of sequins and the pet rabbit can raise the mood on a dismal day (although the rabbit did not find it funny no matter how 'bling' he looked).

Although this won't cure long-term mental health issues and of course is not appropriate in all situations, sometimes a simple shared laugh can make all the difference. If all else fails then excuse yourself for a couple of minutes, go to the toilet, get your phone out and Google 'Cats running into windows' just to lift your mood to enable you to bring more joy to your children.

Wear your pants on your head

A setting I visited had read *Aliens Love Underpants* to their children so the key workers in this particular room wore pants on their heads for the rest of the day. The children thought this was the funniest thing ever. Anna Lucas takes this a step further with her fantastic book *Sir Undercracker*, with a main character who always wears his pants on his head.

Look at your current cohort of children and observe them for moments of laughter. See those children that rarely laugh and see what you can do to help them laugh. In my career I have worked with many children who have barely laughed for their entire lives. When that joyful and sometimes unfamiliar sound bubbles up from a vulnerable child it is one of the most rewarding moments ever.

When you read stories for children make sure you read them with fun and the laughter will follow. Lots of children's stories involve humour and there is a world of difference between a story read with genuine humour and a funny story destroyed by a disinterested reader.

Long live crayons!

My current favourite funny children's book is *The Day the Crayons Came Home*, which is the sequel to the bestseller *The Day the Crayons Quit*", both by Drew Daywalt (author) and Oliver Jeffers (illustrator) (2015). There are some really funny pages in this book (the crayon who has been eaten by a dog for one!) and I love reading it to children. I delivered training for a school recently on World Book Day and one teacher spent the whole day dressed as a crayon in honour of this book.

Let's not be so hard on mischief. Let's acknowledge there is a unique kind of joy that some children experience when being mischievous. Why not celebrate this aspect of childhood rather than brushing it under the carpet and trying to crush it?

You can even do activities that include an element of mischief. We do a lovely series of activities called 'Ninja School'. This can include anything from running around games to climbing things. Standing on one leg and balancing games are also ideal for this. You also need to do sneaking games. One 'mischievous' thing to do is give the children stickers and they have to sneak a sticker onto the back of one of the adults without the adult noticing. Make sure you warn the other adults about the game first and do bear in mind that your younger children may not be that good at being stealthy so try not to react when a child obviously puts a sticker on you. The glee with which some children place their stickers is lovely to see and the game is very empowering, especially for our vulnerable children.

Another game is to have an adult pretending they are a sleeping dragon lying on top of a selection of cuddly toys. The children have to rescue the cuddly toys without waking up the dragon.

Above all let's start to recognise just how important humour is for our entire society and what a precious gift it is if we can support our children through this wonderful developmental process. When planning our experiences for children when was the last time we planned something specifically because it was funny or humorous? Make sure then that this glaring omission is recognised and becomes part of your daily routine for children. Planning should involve humour built in and plenty of opportunities for incongruity and laughter. Support your children to develop humour by acknowledging and validating the humour they have and introducing them to worlds of possibility through new funny experiences. And let's stop making children feel rubbish because they find poo funny, because after all it is funny!

Summary

Humour is a vital social function potentially used almost every day of our lives in one form or another. In addition to providing some much-needed joy, it helps us to overcome adversity, combat stress and supports creative problem solving. We learnt that laughter actually *is* the best medicine, helping us cope with pain and even live longer. We learned that a key aspect of humour is incongruity so we should all wear potatoes on our heads. Even the anticipation of laughter has benefits and when you are laughing you are learning - *literally*! I put forward the suggestion that all teachers should have stand-up comedy training and that mischief is good, poo is joyful and a setting that laughs is a setting that thrives.

6
SEEK AND DESTROY — THE ROBOT TEACHERS ARE COMING!

There have now been trials of robot teachers in primary education and early years. In one such trial the robots had a screen built into their bodies to enable them to show videos to their children. To anyone in the UK this might seem vaguely familiar. Maybe, instead of a much-loved children's show, *Teletubbies* was a bleak look into a dystopian future?

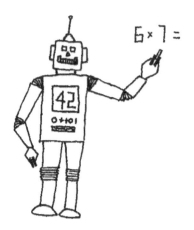

Image 6.1   A robot teacher by F

The main question that needs to be asked of the scientists trialling robot teachers is, 'Have you never watched a *Terminator* film?'

I don't actually believe robots will ever replace human teachers but it does raise some interesting questions. Not only does a robot have instant access to more information than a human being, but with advents in search engine complexity and new semi-AI capabilities they can, within certain limitations, 'understand' complex concepts and pass those concepts on to children.

So, with the right programming a robot teacher could teach the knowledge components and even the level of complexity needed to pass exams. So, if we look at education as merely giving children knowledge then there is an argument that robot teachers could do much of that work.

Not what education is all about?

Of course, that is not what education is really about. I think it is often underestimated just how powerful the impact of a truly good teacher is on a child's life. There is a lot of 'teacher bashing' in the media without really understanding the picture of how challenging teaching really is.

The truth is there are some absolutely amazing teachers out there. I am really privileged to be a guest lecturer for several initial teacher training groups and the level of passion and enthusiasm in these groups is utterly inspiring. I also work with award winning teachers whose commitment to their subject and their understanding of their power to change lives is simply mind blowing.

A dancing dog

I have occasionally delivered keynote speeches at the same venue as Simon James Hunt who is an award-winning primary school teacher. His enthusiasm for teaching is abundantly clear and he is always worth listening to. He taught his class coding by inventing a dance that subsequently went viral and has even written a children's book (*Delilah Rose the Bogey Princess*). Simon James Hunt is amazing, and I don't have a problem with the fact that he is younger, taller, and better looking than me. I am slightly peeved that in addition to teaching his children a dance about coding he has even taught his dog to dance when I can't even get my dog to bring back a ball.

I have accidentally been included in a WhatsApp group set up by the lovely Mike Fleetham of Thinking Classrooms. In this group are a selection of what can only be described as super teachers and head teachers. Every day messages pop up from a group of educators passionately discussing new ways they can better teach their students. Even on a Sunday copious messages pass back and forth discussing how these educators can be the best they can for their children.

I have already mentioned Dave McPartlin who believes in creating the impossible for his children and not forgetting all of the incredible early years practitioners I work with on a daily basis. These people all share something in common. They inspire joy in their children through their passion and enthusiasm for teaching.

Teachers impact on our entire future

I think this hugely important. Just think back to your own childhoods. Think of those all-important decisions we make when we are teenagers for instance. Choosing which subjects to continue with and which subjects to drop are decisions which potentially alter the course of our entire lives. How do we make those all-important choices? On the surface it makes sense that we choose the subjects we have the greater aptitude for. But what makes us have a greater aptitude for one subject rather than for another? Obviously, every young person is different, and we all have different interests and aptitudes. However, when we look back at the teachers for our chosen subjects, I believe it is the teachers who made the subject interesting whose subjects we often have the greatest aptitude for. I will take this a step further in saying that I believe a good teacher can ignite a passion for a subject even in a child who has disengaged. I know from personal experience I did better at subjects with teachers who made the subject fun and worse where it was simply learning facts. Put simply, if a teacher gives us joy in a subject then I believe we will do better in that subject. This means a good teacher will potentially steer the course of our entire lives by making us interested in a subject through their own joy and passion.

So clearly this is something a robot teacher can't do. It may have all of the knowledge instantly accessible in a way that no human can replicate but it doesn't spend its Sundays messaging other robots about new ways to educate. It doesn't have any feelings for a subject either way and so cannot inspire joy, passion and enthusiasm for a subject. It doesn't see a struggling child and instantly change the way it teaches because it relishes the challenge.

But can joy really be a viable approach to education?

I believe that using the model of joy can profoundly impact not just on a child's ability to learn but also their desire to learn more. In short, I believe joy is a fundamental process for learning, unlocking a child's potential and creating a mindset of growth.

Unfortunately, simply believing something is not enough to persuade people to change their thinking. However, one theorist actually takes all of the threads I have discussed in this book and ties them together with an unambiguous message. Joyful education is massively more effective!

Dr Judy Willis is a neuro-educator and educational consultant, and she uses her knowledge of neuroscience to explain exactly why a joyful approach to education is not merely a novel approach, but absolutely essential for children to reach their full potential (Willis, 2007). Looking at various neuroimaging studies and neurochemical research she explains that joyful experiences categorically improve information transmission and storage in the brain. Basically, we are much more likely to remember stuff if the experience is joyful. She also shows that the opposite is true. Stressful conditions actually block information from entering the brain's areas of higher cognitive memory consolidation and storage. These findings are backed up by numerous studies of the human brain.

In addition, joyful classroom experiences cause the brain to release our old friend dopamine, which makes the child feel fantastic. However, Judy takes this a step further by saying that dopamine also stimulates the memory centres of the brain. In addition, dopamine promotes the release of another neurotransmitter, acetylcholine, which actually increases focused attention. So, dopamine doesn't just make the child feel amazing and want to repeat the experience, it also supports the child to retain important information, and increases their focus. Joy helps us to remember stuff!

We are going to be discussing the amygdala (the fear centre of our brain) in the next chapter, but Judy describes something called the 'affective filter', an aspect of the amygdala which filters out information at times of stress. If the affective filter becomes hyper stimulated through stress and anxiety, then new information does not pass through the amygdala to reach the higher cognitive centres of the brain. So, any teaching method that makes the child anxious fundamentally impairs the child's ability to process information because the affective filter actually stops the information reaching the correct parts of the brain for learning. Joyful experiences therefore support the child to think more clearly and crucially help the child to understand what is being taught.

Dr Judy Willis also talks about how 'novel' experiences promote information transmission and increase focus. She describes another aspect of our lower brain, the reticular activating system, which is a filter in the lower brain that focuses attention on novel changes in the child's environment. Unusual and interesting experiences of learning are more likely to pass through the reticular activating system, meaning the child can focus more and is more likely to retain the information. So basically, the tenner in the pocket feeling does not just flood the brain with dopamine but actively enhances learning by increasing our focus and improving memory retention. This means that if learning is stimulating, unusual, fascinating and multisensory it will be significantly more effective.

The best news about all of this is that it is not merely a vague idea that joy is good for children. Judy backs up every one of her observations with established neuroscience and numerous neuroimaging and neurochemical studies. This is not speculation but established fact.

So back to our model of joy. According to Judy Willis:

- Happiness in learning produces dopamine and activates memory

- Engagement and stimulation speed up information transmission and retention

- Emotional safety prevents the affective filter from blocking learning.

Job done!

Not just knowledge

We often forget that teachers do not just teach knowledge. Children model their behaviour on the adults around them and learn much more than facts. Children learn essential social skills, how to cope in a crisis, how to deal with stress and conflict and even how to 'learn' in the first place. In early years we are very aware of our role in modelling behaviours but maybe this gets forgotten as children get older?

Behaviour modelling

Children learn every aspect of their behaviour from the adults around them. This means if an adult shouts at a child and then, for instance, the child is annoyed by another child, then if only one response to stress has been modelled the chances are the child will shout (or use more aggressive behaviour) at the other child. The child may then be sanctioned for the exact behaviour they have just had modelled, causing a child to become confused and stressed because the very behaviours they are having modelled for them are the behaviours they are not allowed to use for themselves.

Behaviour changes after the pandemic

Recently I have been invited to work in several schools because they are struggling with behaviour, especially at lunchtime. A significant number of children had reduced social experiences due to the global pandemic and consequently children may be struggling at lunchtime and break. The head teachers are telling me that children do not play as effectively as previous cohorts, and often conflict breaks out, resulting in a great many sanctions at lunchtime and evident stress in the midday staff.

Another thing a robot teacher can't do is model human behaviours. We can though. If children are struggling with social behaviours, then there is pretty much only one way they can develop these behaviours. Schools have tried increasing sanctions, keeping year groups separate because they can't play together, and one school even shortened their lunchtime by ten minutes because it was identified that a higher proportion of incidents occurred in the final ten minutes.

I really don't understand this last one. Surely even if you shorten the lunchtime, you still have a last ten minutes? All you have done is taken away opportunities for children to play.

If there is an issue with behaviour, often we stop the children having an opportunity for that behaviour rather than giving them the opportunity to grow and develop so that they can cope. If a child is too rough for instance, we stop them from doing boisterous play. If Year 5's and 6's don't play well together we keep them apart. If incidents are happening at lunchtime, we shorten the lunchtime. This is because the emphasis is on stopping the behaviour not supporting children to behave differently. Boisterous play is a classic example.

This type of play is really important as it teaches children their own physical limits. This means that if a child is 'too' rough then often we deprive them of the exact play they need to support them to not be so rough in the first place. Instead of keeping children apart when they cannot behave socially, we need to be modelling social behaviours and teaching children to be able to behave socially in these situations. After all, as an adult you are not always kept apart from people you do not get on with.

I also think we sometimes put behavioural expectations on children that are not only unrealistic but actually the opposite of how the world really works. What I mean by this is that we punish children for doing things when it would not be in the slightest bit appropriate to punish an adult. One of my absolute pet hates is children being told off for needing the toilet.

I need a wee...

I worked in a reception class recently and after break time several children raised their hands and asked to go to the toilet. The class teacher became increasingly exasperated as she told every single child that they should have gone during the break. Those of you who have read my first book will know that the play instinct takes precedence in these situations and so while the child is playing, they do not know that they need to use the toilet. This is because the play behaviours are so important for children that they supersede other bodily issues such as needing the toilet. The first those children are aware that their bladders are full is when they sit on the carpet after break. They are not deliberately trying to make trouble or disrupt the lesson; they simply did not know they needed a wee until they came inside. I explained all this to the teacher and suggested that after break she spends five minutes reminding all the children to go to the toilet.

The other issue is that some children will not dare admit they need the toilet because needing the toilet has now been addressed negatively. There may be some children who will sit in silence whilst desperately needing the toilet. We now know that the added stress and physical discomfort will impair their learning, memory retention and cognition. If they are desperate for the toilet they will not be learning at their full capacity.

Another practice that fundamentally removes the joy from children is keeping them in at break or lunchtime if they have misbehaved or not finished their work. I mentioned this multiple times in my book about play so I won't go into too much detail here. I do still get many requests for the reasons why a child should not have their break taken away from them, so I have created a PDF document with all of the reasons and precedents why a child needs their break and lunchtime and why the practice is potentially counterproductive and unnecessarily cruel. This document can be downloaded from my website (www. inspiredchildren.org.uk). As a personal plea, as someone with ADHD I found the practice to be particularly cruel as a child. The break and lunchtime were a lifeline when trying to remain focused in class and one mistake with behaviour could take that away from me, which was an utterly crushing experience.

All children should have a 1970's childhood?

Back to robot teachers. I often ask my learners on training courses what barriers modern children face in terms of the decline of play. The one thing that comes up time and time again is 'technology'. Numerous studies are showing huge increases in screen-time when compared with previous generations and a fundamental shift in how children play. I often compare my play experiences from the 1970's to those of modern children as a way of illustrating that shift.

I see first-hand just how powerful outdoor play experiences are for children and because these outdoor experiences are often declining, I will often prioritise these experiences over technological experiences. However, this does not mean I am anti-technology. Technology is not going away any time soon and so rather than a knee jerk reaction against this shift in play we need to acknowledge children's play needs are different, that they use technology as part of their play, and this is an important part of their lives. Then we still need to get them outside to play! The truth is we cannot provide children with a 1970's childhood because modern children are different, and society has fundamentally changed.

I think like most things it is about balance. We shouldn't make a teenager feel bad because they enjoy playing *Fortnite* with their friends, but we should balance those opportunities with real-life experiences. We shouldn't ban all technology from our nurseries, but we must make sure children have access to natural resources and environments as well.

What I am trying to say is that as technology is such an important part of our lives it makes sense to sensitively incorporate it into our work with children. In fact, some of my favourite resources are technological ones. I occasionally have resources donated for my work with vulnerable children. One of my all-time favourite resources is some light up bricks from TTS. You shake the bricks and they light up in different colours and you can incorporate them into dens to create some wonderful sensory environments. These bricks make me smile every single time and in fact I get really excited by 'things that light up'.

I am not alone in this weird fascination with light up resources. Every time I bring out the light up bricks, for instance, there will be an audible 'ooh' as they light up. This is regardless of whether I am delivering a children's session or an adult training session, there are just some children and adults for whom light up resources create a very special kind of joy.

A dubious expert

If anyone doubts my credentials to write about 'things that light up' I should point out that I am an avid torch collector (or geek as my friends call me). I have over thirty torches and know the brightness in lumens of each. If you ever meet me in person, I guarantee I will have at least three torches with me and in fact I sometimes mention that I collect torches on training courses in the vain hope that someone will approach me afterwards and admit that they too collect torches. Then I will have made a special friend. This has never happened.

A fundamental force of the universe

So, whether or not you think I have taken things too far with my passion for torches, light has clearly played a huge role in human evolution from the first time we used the stars to navigate to the advent of fire to chase the darkness away and finally to the invention of the electric light bulb. There is something primal and uniquely powerful about our ability to manipulate and produce light. Is it our innate fear of the dark that makes us love light so much? Or is it the tiny bit of us that desires the power of a god to push back the darkness?

As one of the most fundamental and powerful forces in the universe our human capacity to manipulate light brings a feeling of empowerment to even our very young children. The ability to wield light, to instantly illuminate things and bring clarity is universally empowering and if you give a child a torch you will see this empowerment.

In Bob Hughes' *Taxonomy of Play Types* (2002) he describes 'recapitulative play" as play that displays aspects of human evolutionary history. This is arguably one of the most difficult of the 16 play types for modern children to engage in and yet I believe the human fascination for light and light-up objects does just this. Some of our most modern and 'technological' toys actually support very primitive aspects of humanity.

The tenner in the pocket again!

What makes children continuously enthralled by our light up resources? I think there is something wonderfully surprising about these kinds of resources and we now know what that surprising happiness does to our reward system. Copious amounts of enhanced dopamine, the tenner in the pocket feeling or the first pop of the bubble feeling! I also know that even though I have now seen those bricks light up hundreds of times I still smile when it happens.

Alien abduction

The only exception to this is when I went over a speed bump whilst driving home at night. The entire box of bricks lit up, filling my rear-view mirror with a multicoloured glow. For a brief instance my brain could not understand what it was seeing, having completely forgotten the bricks were in the van. I was just coming to the conclusion that I was about to be abducted by aliens when I remembered the bricks.

Fear of the dark

Light is not just empowering and joyful though. It is also comforting and reassuring, representing safety and security for countless generations of humanity. After all, as all children know, it is not the dark that is frightening but the monsters who live in the dark, and the one thing monsters fear is light. From those earliest days of using fire to scare away predators, to the comfort of a night light in a child's room to help them sleep, light represents safety. This fundamental aspect of joy that is so essential is provided by simple technology.

Image 6.2   A monster being scared by a torch by F

Also, let's not forget that in Simon Nicholson's theory of loose parts play he cites playing with forces as an integral part of enriched play environments (Nicholson, 1971). Playing with light and shadow is hugely beneficial for children and intrinsically rich in terms of spatial awareness. The fact that a shadow becomes bigger the nearer to the light source is innately mathematical and simple shadow play with children can help embed complex scientific concepts whilst providing them with joyful explorations. It is also a fantastic way to make stories come to life.

Let there be light…

So, am I saying that we should always use light up resources? Of course not. Equally I am not saying that outdoor experiences with natural resources can ever be replaced by technology. What I am saying is that there are unique moments of joy to be had through use of light up resources, empowering our children to manipulate one of the fundamental forces of the universe and unleash their inner god.

Embracing tech

Interestingly, when we look at those examples of amazing teachers, they are not resisting technology but embracing it. Simon Hunt uses dance moves to learn all about coding and is passionate about new and interesting uses of technology in the classroom. Mike Fleetham's group chats for hours about advances in technology and their positive uses in the classroom. They recently had a hugely in-depth discussion about the latest advances in search engine AI. They were not merely reiterating the scare mongering comments in the media but looking at innovative new uses for this technology in a classroom environment.

An overly enthusiastic ferret

Simon James Hunt likes to take photographs at conferences. He then displays these on the big screen during lunchtime for instance. In every single picture he has ever taken of me, I look like an overly enthusiastic ferret. These are then shown in glorious detail to everyone else at the conference.

So maybe the robot teachers are not such an appalling idea. If the best human teachers are embracing technology and looking at new and interesting ways to apply this in the classroom, then maybe there is a role for the robot teacher. After all, the robot teacher can store and access more information than a human ever could. However, the aspects of learning the robots excel at, passing on information, were never the most important aspects of teaching in the first place. Robot teachers may one day have their place and may even alleviate some of the more tiresome aspects of teaching, allowing the human teachers to focus on what is really important. Let the robot teachers cover the knowledge bits of learning and let the human teachers do all the really good bits. Let the human teachers inspire passion and wonder, support our children to become pro-social human beings through modelling social behaviours and above all give our children joy because only when children have a joy in learning can they truly reach their potential.

What does this look like in practice?

OK, so we know that joyful experiences of learning flood the brain with addictive biochemicals making the child crave learning. We know that joyful experiences of learning activate children's curiosity and fundamentally change the shape of their brain to engage with more learning. We also know that negative experiences of learning disengage a child and make it increasingly difficult for them to learn to their full potential. In the next chapter we are going to look at exactly what anxiety does to the brain but suffice it to say that it is the absolute opposite of learning. So, what this looks like in practice is really obvious. Children must experience joy in learning if they are to reach their full potential.

There doesn't seem to be any ambiguity in the research and there is certainly no evidence I have found that equates negative experiences with any kind of academic progress. So, it looks like the amazing teachers have it right. They are less focused on knowledge and much more about the experience of learning. They see a child who is struggling as a challenge, not in terms of their behaviour but to find ways of teaching that will engage even our hardest to reach children. The awesome Judy Willis states that there is not a single neuroimaging study that demonstrates any negative effects of a joyful approach to learning (Willis, 2007). So, if a concordance of evidence supports a joyful approach and not one shred of evidence supports its opposite, then what are we waiting for?

There is a bit of a paradox here. An argument could be made that positive methods of teaching do not work when faced with a cohort of resistant and potentially negatively behaved children. However, children who feel more positive and have a higher level of self-worth and confidence are significantly more likely to exhibit pro-social behaviour. They are also more likely to engage with learning. So rather than making the learning experience unpleasant for children who are struggling we should be embedding joy in every aspect of teaching, which in turn gives children a better chance for pro-social behaviour. In almost every conversation with parents they cite the good teachers as the ones who make the subject fun for their students and support the child when they are struggling. I have an awful lot of conversations with parents. When I deliver my parent play training, naturally parents want to talk about their own children. I therefore have thousands of anecdotal examples of how a good teacher, one who makes the subject fun and supports children who are struggling, changes lives. I also have numerous anecdotal examples of the opposite and how catastrophic this is for our children. Without realising it the amazing teachers are applying the principles of joy to the everyday experiences of their children. They are ensuring the learning is fun and making children happy. They are then making the learning interesting and stimulating, ensuring the highest possible level of engagement and above all they are making children feel safe, important and worthwhile.

The best thing about using a model of joy in a classroom environment is that even if it doesn't work to improve learning, you have not fundamentally harmed the children. Other approaches, if misused, can actually raise anxiety levels which will significantly impair learning.

Another counter argument to the joyful approach is that as children progress through education, the increasing demands on a teacher's time mean that they simply cannot implement a joy based approach and still get through the amount of work that needs to be covered.

I fully understand this, and I know that teachers put in many extra hours of work outside of the classroom just to meet the requirements of their courses. However, if we accept the research (and there is a lot of it) that children learn slower if they are anxious or unstimulated, then taking extra time to focus on well-being might not leave children behind at all. The time spent to improve well-being is a sound investment for future progress because only when children feel safe, valued and stimulated can they learn at their optimum rate. So rather than piling on even more stress to children who are already struggling, we need to take time to work on our children's well-being because only then can we truly support children to learn.

I think as educators we need to acknowledge that sometimes the learning outcomes will need to be thrown out. We all have bad days, days when we can't concentrate or when we feel particularly vulnerable. Sometimes we need to recognise that our children are struggling and be confident enough to stop what we are doing and run outside for a big old game of leapfrog.

She flattens me every time!

A reception class I delivered an inset day for had issues with children who struggled with formal learning. They would fidget, lose concentration and misbehave, which had a knock-on effect on other children and staff members. After I had delivered my training about the benefits of play, and during one particularly challenging session, a teacher in frustration shouted, 'Stop! Leapfrog break!' The children and staff all went outside to play leapfrog. The teacher was astounded by the difference in the children when they returned to the classroom. They were more engaged, less badly behaved and fundamentally in a better state for learning. The

(Continued)

teacher confided to me that her classroom assistant was a large lady who would inadvertently flatten her every time she leapfrogged. However, far from being negative this showed all the children it was OK to get it wrong and it usually all ended up in a big pile up on the floor! They now use physical play throughout the day to support the children to learn more effectively.

So, as educators we need to do what the robots can never do, which is to inspire joy, passion and enthusiasm in our children. We need to make children feel safe and important and be there with them on their learning journey, not merely as a repository for facts but as a willing partner, exploring the fascinating world together. This journey starts in the early years, and we should be supporting and feeding our children's genuine enthusiasm for the world and all the fantastic things in it. We should never be steering the child down the path of disinterest simply because we don't find the same things interesting.

Astronomy for early years

I get many odd requests for training. One of the more unusual was a nursery setting who asked me to deliver astronomy training. This was because they had several children who loved everything about space, so they wanted to be more knowledgeable about the subject to better support and engage the children. Just think about this for a second. Despite all of the expense and effort it takes to make sure a nursery has all the statutory training required, they actually paid me to deliver astronomy training as additional continuing professional development (CPD). They did this because the practitioners had a passion for supporting their children's passions! The training was hugely fun to deliver and had the knock-on effect of rekindling my love of space and astronomy (yes, we did build a giant rocket out of cardboard boxes!).

This is what I am talking about. You don't need to be interested in space to genuinely inspire and support children's interests but if you are willing to go on the learning journey with your children you can share moments of genuine awe and wonder. The added bonus is that if we can support our children's passions regardless of our own preconceptions, we might just learn something ourselves.

We also need to acknowledge that technology is here to stay and is not automatically something to be resisted. There are some amazing uses of technology and some quite negative ones. Like everything in life, we need a balance. I don't often use TV screens in nursery settings and never to watch actual TV because the children are statistically likely to have those screen-based experiences outside of the setting. So, in order to provide a balance, I provide more outdoor experiences. I do, however, use USB microscopes to look at mini beasts and plants, etc. I use light up bricks, glowing potions and wind-up torches in dens.

Similarly, I don't have games consoles in afterschool clubs because the chances are that children will have access to this technology outside of the club. Therefore, providing games consoles to children is not a balanced approach. I do however use things like Lego Mindstorms, digital photography, animation and DJ software in my afterschool clubs because these are experiences they may not be able to access outside the setting. I also include lots of outdoor and boisterous play because I know this is going to be of the most benefit.

Real life *Minecraft*

I know I said I didn't use games consoles in afterschool clubs but that is not entirely true. On one of our Autism spectrum disorder (ASD) groups, we do support the children to play *Minecraft* because it is extremely comforting, highly creative and actually encourages social behaviours because they love to talk about their *Minecraft* experiences. However, it is all about balance and so we occasionally encourage the young people to play 'real' *Minecraft*. We provide an unfeasibly huge amount of cardboard boxes and bits of material for water and fire and we create some really enormous structures. The young people absolutely love the session. This does not mean that they always prefer 'real' *Minecraft* but that the real-life experiences are a great way to balance the screen-based experiences whilst still following their interests and passions.

So how do we know what the positive uses for technology are and when we need to restrict it? Well, our equation for joy comes in really handy here. If children are full of happiness whilst engaging with technology, if they are genuinely stimulated rather than just killing time and if they feel fundamentally safe then the experience is likely to be a positive one. This does not mean that children should be doing this to the exclusion of all the other wonderful things, but it means that their time engaging with the technology is a positive one. If, however, the experience is engaged in with a blank face, an absence of happiness and is accompanied by anger and frustration or even a complete lack of emotion then it is probably not that good for our children and maybe we need to find something else or balance the experience with real-life experiences.

An exploding star!

In the constellation of Orion is a star called Betelgeuse. This star is a red giant and is over a thousand times bigger than our sun, which is itself pretty mind bogglingly huge. The really exciting thing about Betelgeuse is that it is now at the end of its life. This means that any minute now it could explode in a such a cataclysmic fashion that the resultant supernova will be seen from the earth. In the daytime! Any time now we could have a brand-new light in our skies. Go on, go outside right now and check. Of course, 'any minute now' could be thousands of years but it is still pretty exciting. Even more exciting is it might already have happened, and we are just waiting for the light to reach the earth. How do I know all of this? Because one nursery requested astronomy training as CPD for their staff.

We also need to remember that at our current level of technology a robot can never model behaviours for children. This is arguably one of the most important things we ever do and fundamentally changes how a child views the world. We need to think about what children are actually assimilating from our modelling and what traits and behaviours we want our children to learn from us. If we don't stop to think about our social impact, we could be reinforcing negative emotions and behaviour patterns without giving our children useful responses to challenge and stress. I don't think a robot will ever be able to do this and I think this alone means that we absolutely cannot ever replace human teachers.

So, at first glance it seems like robot teachers are a really dark path to a dystopian future (Alexa, play sinister music). Actually though, if we look at them not as replacing human teachers but as a way of outsourcing some of the burden of teaching, they could be a positive influence on education. They could allow human teachers to focus on what is really important, providing joyful experiences for our children. By working with positive technology and supporting children to experience all of the really cool things about it, whilst at the same time making sure we provide the right balance of outdoor, real life and imaginary/creative experiences then education could be something really powerful.

Summary

So, we have learned that robot teachers can never replace human teachers and our role as an educator is providing joyful, stimulating experiences for our children. We learned that a joyful approach to education is backed up by a concordance of evidence and that Judy Willis is a legend. We also learned that I always look like a ferret on photos and that Betelgeuse could explode any minute. Most importantly we learned that as educators we need to share and be part of our children's learning journey, sharing their discoveries and their passions, and supporting them to see the amazingness of the world (Alexa, play joyful music).

7

WHO STOLE OUR JOY?

Up to now we have been discussing the vital role of joy in every aspect of a child's development and well-being. In this chapter we will be looking at what happens when that joy is absent from a child's life. If I'm being honest, I have been putting off writing this chapter. The subject matter is potentially extremely upsetting, and it would be much easier to write the whole book about the positive aspects of joy so that reading the book is in itself a joyful experience. However, the truth is that a significant number of children do not experience joy in their lives. I work with children for whom the concept of joy is almost completely unknown and learning about those children's life experiences can be harrowing. In this chapter I am going to paint a very bleak picture of some children's life experiences and the appalling impact of a life without joy. I would forgive anyone at this point if they wished to skip this chapter entirely and join us for the next chapter when (hopefully) things have taken a more joyful turn.

If you are still with me, it is because, like me, you believe that we need to know about the potential damage being done to some of our children. Only by being aware of this can we do our best to ensure we do not repeat these mistakes and support our most vulnerable children.

Anyone who has experienced depression or anxiety may have occasionally experienced a sense of complete withdrawal where it becomes almost impossible to do anything. There is a feeling of such numbness or disconnectedness that it becomes unbearable to engage in anything. There are no hopes, no aspirations and in fact very little thought at all, as it feels as if we have fundamentally shut down. Some people describe a sense of being a passenger in their own bodies, dimly aware of their surroundings but unable to make their body do anything. Other people describe being stuck in a loop in their brain, the same thoughts repeating over and over. In short there is a complete absence of joy in our lives.

Psychologists may describe this state as dissociation. This is the state the brain enters where flight or fight have failed, and the brain begins to shut down as a last defence. Perhaps most upsettingly, this is the state the brain enters when all hope is absent. If you ever watch a nature documentary this dissociative state occurs when the antelope has already been brought down by the lion and has no chance to escape. In the last few moments before death the antelope's brain shuts down and it stops struggling. Prolonged anxiety or fear can induce this dissociative state in our children and compromise every aspect of their well-being and development. Because dissociation represents a fundamental 'checking out' of the brain, any child experiencing this state will find all aspects of learning critically difficult because their brain is not able to process information. This state is catastrophic for children's well-being.

Mental health issues are not weakness

There seems to be a myth in this country that mental health problems are somehow a weakness and that anyone struggling with depression or anxiety needs to 'toughen-up'. Nothing could be further from the truth. If you experience depression or anxiety, then every single thing you do becomes significantly more difficult. I like to compare this to watching a race. If you watch two people racing, you might assume that the one who crosses the finishing line first has worked the hardest. It is only when you understand that the other person is running against a gale force wind that you realise how hard it was for that person to cross the finish line at all. Anyone with anxiety or depression will have days when everything they do is much harder, as if they are trying to run into a gale. This does not make them weaker but some of the strongest people on the planet.

Not fit for purpose

One of the problems is that parts of our brain are no longer fit for purpose. The amygdala, or fear centre of our brain, is part of the primitive limbic system, shared with all mammals and arguably about 200,000,000 years old. Its purpose is to increase our survival chances by activating in dangerous or frightening situations and giving us enhanced capabilities to survive a physical threat. Amygdala activation creates biochemical and physiological changes to help us survive potentially threatening situations:

- Our breathing becomes faster and shallower to rapidly oxygenate our blood
- Our heart rate then increases to move the oxygenated blood quickly to our muscles
- This increases our speed and strength and prepares us to escape or fight a threat
- Muscles tense in preparation for physical action (fight or flight)
- The muscles in our hands tense in preparation of forming a fist to punch an attacker
- Our focus becomes much narrower, focusing on the threat at hand, ignoring distractions until the danger has passed
- Non-essential brain functions are 'disconnected'
- The brain floods with cortisol and other stress hormones
- The entire brain and body become ready to fight or flee a threat.

Now, whilst these physiological changes are extremely helpful at evading or surviving a physical threat, they also have negative repercussions such as additional strain on our heart, aggressive behaviour and poor mood. This is in addition to the negative effects of stress hormones like cortisol. In the primitive world these negatives are an acceptable trade-off because the short-term survival benefits outweigh the negative impact. However, in the modern world only a tiny proportion of experiences that trigger our amygdala are actual physical dangers. For every other occurrence the amygdala is no longer fit for purpose.

No more cave bears!

The problem is that the world 200,000,000 years ago was a very different place. Many of the things that make us anxious now are much less obvious than the clear threats from primitive times. Social anxiety for instance activates the amygdala but there is no obvious threat to run from or punch. We therefore experience all of the negative impact of activating our amygdala but with no outlet.

Social anxiety, maths phobia and even school anxiety will trigger amygdala responses that are no longer fit for purpose and become overwhelmingly negative for children without any of the short-term survival benefits.

So, stress, anxiety and fear cause an amygdala response, flooding us with the stress hormone cortisol making us more aggressive and preparing us for fight or flight. When the brain finds itself trapped and flight or fight have failed or are not useful, the brain begins to dissociate. Because modern stress factors are often less tangible, then fight or flight responses are more likely to be redundant. This increases the chances of a child beginning to dissociate.

One often overlooked example of the amygdala not being fit for purpose is that the fingers of an anxious child will become tense and stiff. This means they will find holding a pencil and writing to be more difficult and the control over their finger movements will be impaired. This could make the experience of writing itself a source of anxiety which will further impair the child's ability to write.

Driving anxiety?

I drive all over the UK but find driving in London to be particularly stressful. I arrived at the Childcare & Education Expo recently and found that removing my hands from the steering wheel was actually painful because I had become so tense during my journey that my fingers had formed rigid claws.

If a child suffers from school anxiety, they will trigger their amygdala by simply being in the classroom. This means they are trapped in a fearful situation with no recourse. Their heart rate increases and their muscles tense. Then with no recourse of fight or flight they may begin to dissociate which will critically impact on learning and development.

Forgotten sandwiches

Very few people who know me will be aware that I suffer from social anxiety. They assume because I deliver keynote speeches to hundreds of people and am always talking and telling funny stories that I must be extremely confident socially. In fact, the opposite is true. I don't feel overly anxious talking to large groups of people but in smaller social situations I can become extremely anxious. I try to fill every silence with something humorous and the more anxious I get the less funny I become. One peculiar aspect of my social anxiety is that if put under pressure, complete rubbish will just come out of my mouth. Now don't get me wrong, I am genuinely an honest person and am not trying to be dishonest, but sometimes anxiety just makes me blurt out random things that might not necessarily be true. I recently employed a new member of staff who speaks very slowly and leaves long pauses. Now there is absolutely nothing wrong with this at all and she is a fantastic worker and really lovely. However, for some reason this makes me anxious. As a person with ADHD I now know it is rude to finish peoples sentences but I can't help my thoughts running ahead and then waiting for the speaker to catch up with my brain. This waiting is what I find triggering. She recently said to me, 'Well Ben... I've forgotten my lunch'. There was then a long silence before I blurted out, 'Yes, I have too!' I hadn't! I then had to work for six hours, very hungry and not able to eat my sandwiches because if I did, I would look like a weirdo who lies about his sandwiches!

Negative experiences fundamentally impair learning

I have talked about this in previous chapters, but it bears repeating. AN ANXIOUS CHILD IS FUNDAMENTALLY LESS ABLE TO LEARN. We need to be repeating this to ourselves as a mantra because if we ever want a child to reach their full potential, they simply cannot do this if they are experiencing fear or anxiety. This is not a conscious choice, or weakness or laziness, or in any way the child's fault. It is simply how the brain works.

In all mammals, anger, fear and anxiety cause the amygdala to trigger, creating all of the physiological responses mentioned earlier. In order to preserve life, the focus of the mammal turns purely to the immediate threat to the exclusion of all other considerations. In short, the amygdala takes control allowing the mammal to act on 'animal instinct' to avoid a threat. What this looks like in the brain is a focus on the limbic system responses whilst unnecessary upper brain functions are effectively 'disconnected'. In your dog or cat this disconnection of upper brain function manifests in aggressive and or fleeing behaviours and an overall deterioration of mood.

Big brains

Without being rude to dogs and cats, they have a lot less upper brain to begin with so the impact of this 'disconnection' is less obvious. Humans are different though. Around 800,000 to 200,000 years ago there was a bizarre mutation in our ancestors' brains causing the frontal lobes to grow much bigger. This growth was so significant that the human skull grew to accommodate this mutated growth. In short, we became 'big brain' mammals which is why unlike other mammals our skulls are so flat and round. However, the Amygdala is still in there from 200,000,000 years ago doing its best to protect us. It still has the same physiological effect regardless of how big and swollen our upper brain has become and it still effectively disconnects those upper brain functions in times of stress. So, in your dog or cat the bit that is disconnected, whilst still unbelievably complex, is comparatively quite small. In humans both the bits of brain and the impact is huge. We believe that our self-awareness and consciousness are in the upper brain. Communication and language, imagination and creativity are all upper brain. What about mathematics, literacy, decision making and problem solving? Upper brain again. Even our moral code, ethics and empathy are upper brain. These are the very functions that are impaired when we are scared, anxious or angry because the bits of our brain responsible are effectively disconnected.

The amygdala hijacks our upper brain to make us act more on animal instinct to save us from an immediate threat. This impairs every single bit of our brain that makes us human. Every aspect of our learning and development and even our morals and ethics are impaired when we are anxious, afraid and angry.

I really hope this is making sense because I think it is vital that we know about this stuff. It calls into question many of the entrenched ideas still prevalent in education in the UK because any practice that makes a child anxious will impair the child from learning at their full potential and stop the one thing that is the sole purpose of an education establishment in the first place, which is to educate.

It is also worth remembering that short- and long-term memory retention are also impaired by stress. The affective filter ensures that if the amygdala is activated through fear, then vital information no longer reaches the upper brain. To me this is a literal no brainer. If we make children feel anxious, they cannot learn to their full potential so any practice in education that for any reason makes children feel anxious, scared or angry should be stopped immediately.

Cortisol is bad news

It is also worth noting that cortisol, a stress hormone, is critically bad for us. In the short-term it is helpful in facing threats because it causes several physiological changes to help us in a dangerous situation. It increases blood sugar levels, to give more energy for fight or flight. It supresses natural functions that are not essential in a threat situation and this can include the digestive system and even growth processes. It even enhances the healing process in anticipation of injury. In the short-term low levels of cortisol can actually be beneficial and even improve our ability to focus.

If cortisol leaves our body after the threat has subsided, then under normal conditions the harm it does should not be significant. The problem comes when we are exposed to cortisol for extended periods of time with no respite. Extended periods of fear and anxiety will ensure that cortisol stays in our system, and this results in an extremely long list of negative side-effects. When injected into rats for instance, we are talking about a rat having a really bad day, experiencing almost every symptom of depression. These symptoms include poor sleep, digestive problems, startle responses, muscle aches and pains, headaches, increased aggression and dissociation.

It is the effect on the brain which is most worrying. Extended periods of increased cortisol levels can result in damage to the hippocampus which is an area of the brain vital for our long-term memory function. This is because cortisol is acidic in nature and causes physical burning damage to the brain. Other studies show that elevated cortisol levels over a prolonged time period can damage the brain's pre-frontal cortex. This part of the brain is responsible for many crucial functions and is essential for focused attention and executive function, cognitive processes that allow you to plan, organise and solve problems. This part of the brain may also be important for empathy and our ability to control impulses. In short, the hippocampus and the pre-frontal cortex are parts of the brain we really don't want to mess with if we want our children to thrive. So, increased cortisol levels, if left unchecked, can cause physical damage to the brain, impairing learning and fundamentally undermining the child's ability to thrive (Colino, 2022). No setting working with children should ever contemplate methods of working with children that have even the slightest chance of physically damaging a child's brain.

The biggest problem of all is that children experiencing elevated cortisol levels are more likely to exhibit negative behaviour and are significantly less able to learn. This may mean that the stressful factors repeat themselves over and over again as the child repeatedly misbehaves and fails to achieve learning objectives. This is a child who is stuck in a cycle of stress and is in a very dark place. They are now at high risk of physical damage to their brains which will further impair learning.

Training terrors

My social anxiety also makes training a potentially stressful experience for me. I don't mean delivering training but being a trainee. One practice that raises my anxiety levels is, 'Let's go round the room and say our names and a bit about ourselves!'

To me this 'circle of death' is really triggering, waiting for my turn and not knowing what nonsense is going to come out of my mouth. I also find ice breakers, role play and 'getting to know you games' particularly challenging.

When I started training many years ago, I was expected to use all these methods on my training. I soon noticed that I was not the only one who hates these aspects of training. Now I manage my own company I can train how I would like to be trained, and this means no icebreakers, no role-play and never, ever going round the room making everyone speak!

So, just like with my adult training sessions the key to education, as an absolute baseline, is for children to feel safe. This can then be the platform for joy which is the complete opposite of the negative emotions associated with anger, fear and anxiety. Maybe, then, we need to relook at our initial equation for joy, placing emotional safety as the platform for all other aspects of joy. I now see emotional safety as the launchpad for all of the other aspects of joy. It doesn't matter how amazing the rocket is, without a launchpad it will fail to launch. Emotional safety is that launchpad.

Home neurons

I previously mentioned a child who would sigh when he arrived at the after-school club. His name is Jack, and we will hear more about him later. He would throw his bag into the corner and sigh audibly. This was because to a child who does not feel fundamentally safe at school or at home, the after-school club can be the only place in their entire life they can truly relax. Clearly Jack felt more at home at our setting than he did even in his actual home.

There is something really special about this feeling of 'home' that ties in completely with the picture of joy I am trying to piece together. In our nurseries there is a moment when the child overcomes their initial unease and begins to feel at home. This can be on day one, or it can take weeks, but when children run into our settings without a backwards glance then we have truly created a new home for our children.

Once again neuroscience may have a potential reason for this. It turns out we have specific brain cells which activate when we are in a safe space, and

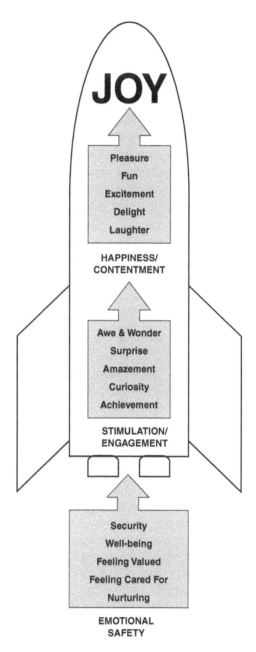

Figure 7.1   Emotional safety rocket

which actually calm down our amygdala responses to stress. This means that in a place we feel is like a home we automatically feel less stress, produce less of the toxic stress hormones and generally feel better about everything.

These neurons have been nicknamed 'home' neurons because they identify when we are at 'home'. Just like laughter though, they actually activate in anticipation of being in a safe space. This means if we are in a home we feel safe, in the home neurons will activate when we are a few streets away in anticipation of us being at home.

This may be one reason why moving home is considered one of the most stressful experiences because we become fundamentally untethered from a space where our home neurons can activate. It also explains why it is so stressful when our home, for whatever reason, no longer feels like a home. This can be because there is another person in our home who does not make us feel safe or even simple things such as a water leak or renovation work. When working with refugee children this is particularly important as they are potentially thousands of miles away from their home and sometimes even their family. This creates an intense sense of dislocation and a pervading feeling of anxiety that we must work very hard to overcome. We also need to remember that refugee children haven't just been uprooted from their homes. They are also taken away from their familiar school, shops, streets and in fact every certainty in their lives.

A calm quiet space

Several years ago, I worked with a young refugee girl who had lost both parents whilst fleeing her country. Her foster carer was extremely worried as the child did not seem to sleep anywhere near enough and what little sleep she did have was broken by frequent crying. Her eyes were red, and she looked absolutely exhausted all the time. As if that were not enough, she was constantly startled by small noises or fast movement. We now know that excessive cortisol levels significantly impact on sleep and an overactive amygdala will cause startle reactions. We were very fortunate to have a sensory room in the nursery where it was much quieter, darker and cool even on a hot day. I spent a long time with the child in our sensory room playing with finger puppets and some sensory resources. Over the next few days, she would not venture out into the main room but became more and more absorbed in the resources and play we shared in the sensory room. About a week later she looked up from the toys, moved towards me and lay her head on my lap. She fell instantly asleep. I sat still for over an hour, not daring to move for fear of waking her up. The next day the same thing happened but this time with another member of staff. This became a regular occurrence and then something even more special happened. The next time I was in the sensory room with her, she fell asleep but after her sleep she held my hand and led me into the main room so she could investigate the toys in there.

This is hugely important for settings working with children. This means if we want our children to feel as safe and anxiety free as possible, we need to make sure our environment activates their home neurons so that they feel automatically less anxious. If we get this right our children will start to feel less anxious at the mere anticipation of coming to our setting.

Home and garden

I recently worked in a reception class and they had remodelled their outdoor space to resemble a garden rather than a school playground. It had real grass rather than an artificial surface and a sandpit as well as various trees and shrubs. It also had a playhouse and a mud kitchen and all of the play resources had been subtly integrated to create the look and feel of a lovely garden. I sat observing children playing barefoot on the grass and I cannot describe how calming the space felt. The children were so completely comfortable in their garden that the adults needed barely any input as the children explored and experimented freely with the resources. I think perhaps that was the most fascinating thing about this 'home' garden. Because the children felt so safe and joyful the level of their own self-directed learning was extremely high. Not only was their level of engagement high, but their social interactions were also incredibly rich and positive. Children were negotiating, taking turns and sharing resources. Quite simply the calming nature of the environment was supporting accelerated social and cognitive development because the children felt at home. Their 'home' neurons were in full effect keeping their amygdala responses under control and significantly enhancing their joyful experiences. I wonder if we have 'garden' neurons too?

So maybe this explains the children who can talk freely when we are in a cardboard box? Maybe something about a cardboard box or similar den activates our home neurons, lowering our amygdala response and making us less likely to be anxious? All of our cardboard boxes are now purchased from a removal firm as we no longer have the time to source free ones. Coincidentally, the removal firm's strap line is *'Removing your stress!'*, which is written in large letters on the boxes. This means that we have children sitting in cardboard boxes literally *'removing their stress'*.

Just clowning around

OK, it's time we got to the important bit which is of course insulting clowns. I have had several negative encounters with clowns in my career and perhaps the worst was in a children's theme park in the West Midlands (I won't name which). This particular clown was wandering around the park throwing a ball at children's faces and shouting, 'catch', making them jump in alarm. Of course, the ball was hilariously on elastic so it would bounce back to his hand without hitting the child. I will pause here to let the laughter die away. The problem was that one of our children had much faster reflexes than the clown anticipated. Neville actually caught the ball before it could snap back to the clown. This caused the clown to let go of the elastic, so Neville casually tossed the ball into a fountain and said, 'catch'. The clown then tried to physically attack Neville whilst swearing at the top of his voice whilst I attempted to hold him back. I still remember stepping on his overly large shoes as I tried to wrestle him away from Neville.

OK, so I know that was a silly (but sadly true) story, but this highlights something potentially very damaging for our vulnerable children. There are some adults who feel the need to be 'mean' to children. I do not know what motivates this behaviour, but some adults seem to feel that children are worthy of contempt simply by being children. Maybe it is their own sense of disempowerment that causes them to pick on what they consider an easier target, or maybe for some reason they genuinely don't like children. They become outraged if children show initiative or even the slightest spark of rebellion and seem to make it their mission to make children feel as worthless as possible. The way they talk, their attitude and body language and their outright disrespect of children make their feelings very clear, especially to the children around them. Children are seen as at best an inconvenience and at worst something detestable and worthless.

Teasing and banter are not harmless

I cannot tell you how many times I have heard adults casually undermine children in the name of teasing and banter. Teasing and banter, no matter how innocuous it seems, can be devastating for children.

I realise I am perhaps on shaky ground here. There are many adults who work with children who use teasing and banter on a daily basis and see no harm in this whatsoever. The argument being that children need to toughen-up and it's just a bit of fun.

I don't want to be ambiguous here. I want to be absolutely clear that teasing and banter is absolutely catastrophic for vulnerable children. I have lost count of the number of times well-meaning and even 'nice' adults have ripped the confidence from a child in the name of banter. I also know that the child who laughs hardest at the teasing is sometimes the child who it hurts the most.

Teasing can be catastrophic

At the beginning of the book, I mentioned a project I run with adopted children and their families. The lovely thing about this project is that I see the families progress and grow together. One child has been coming to the sessions for a while and has been steadily growing in confidence. At the last session, however, he seemed a little quieter and so I asked his dad if he was OK. The dad informed me that he had experienced a major setback. The child's confidence had been growing and so he went on an outdoor pursuits trip with the school. This was a big deal to the child. During the trip an instructor teased the child for not being 'brave' enough to do the high wires and in front of the whole group called him a coward. After all, it's only harmless banter and it doesn't bother children, does it? Except in this case the child went home, got a carving knife out of the kitchen drawer and attempted to cut his wrists.

I have the permission of the parents to share this story as they want to prevent it happening to other children.

I know this is an extreme case and deeply upsetting. I also know some genuinely lovely people who regularly tease children in an affectionate way and believe it does no harm. I promise, I am not trying to be critical and if I'm being honest, I have even been guilty of this behaviour myself. What I am saying is that we can never be 100 per cent sure we are not hurting a child if we use teasing and banter so let's stop taking the risk. Let's show our children a better role model. Also, let's remember that children get all of their behaviour models from the adults around them so all we are really teaching children is how to tease other children. This is not an exercise in 'toughening-up' but a repeated cycle of negativity that fundamentally removes the joy from some children's lives.

Big ears

I once worked with a child whose nickname was 'Jug'. Why? Big ears. Even his parents called him 'Jug', saying 'He doesn't mind, do you Jug?' Jug would dutifully grin and say that it didn't bother him. Except once again it did. I know this because we subsequently banned nicknames at the setting. There was resistance to this move even among the staff as they felt that banter was an important way to bond with the children. However, they all soon discovered an improvement in the whole atmosphere of the setting. The child was still 'Jug' at school and 'Jug' at home but he was Daniel at our after-school club. It made such a difference to Daniel that you could see it in every aspect of his behaviour, confidence and happiness.

You don't actually need teasing and banter to engage with children. You can be yourself and form bonds with children based on caring and nurturing rather than on making children laugh at another child's expense. Remember that teasing by adults tends to be one way. The adult can tease the child, but the child does not necessarily have the vocabulary and life experience to tease back. Or the adult who teases is usually in a position of power that makes it impossible for a child to respond because they themselves feel disempowered. Most often it seems harmless, and in some cases it might be, but because you never know then we need to find another way to interact.

There is also a view that you are somehow preparing children for life by teasing them because they are going to get teased by other people. This is a flawed approach for several reasons. Firstly, the fact that children may get teased outside of our setting is a reason to avoid teasing, not do it more. If we know anything about working with vulnerable children, we know they need to have positive experiences in their lives to outweigh the negative. Secondly, we also know that giving children negative experiences does not better prepare children for negative experiences but has the opposite effect. You are not toughening children up by teasing them but undermining their confidence and making them feel disempowered and potentially worthless. You are also teaching them how to tease others and promoting a cycle of negativity which is almost guaranteed to lead to negative behaviour not just for the child but potentially for the setting as a whole. In short you are almost guaranteeing negative behaviour because you are reinforcing a cycle of disempowerment and modelling teasing as the only way to address that disempowerment. It is no coincidence that when I am asked to visit a setting due to behaviour issues, I often see the adults teasing children.

Teasing songs

I was recently asked to support an afterschool club because their children lacked confidence and did not want to try anything new. So, looking at our model of joy, clearly their happiness was lower, and their levels of engagement were lower. As for the underpinning aspect of safety, well it turns out that this setting had a song they would sing if a child fell over, failed at something or did something embarrassing. It was actually quite impressive and funny to see all the adults singing and dancing to a song specifically to take the mickey out of the children. It was done with big smiles and there was genuine affection for the children and all of the children laughed and joined in with the song. This song had been sung by workers at the setting for years and in fact some of the staff had actually been children who came through the setting and now worked there as adults. They had the song sung at them in their turn and it 'never did them any harm'. Not one member of staff in that setting had made the connection. They could not work out why their children seemed so underconfident. You would not believe the resistance to my suggestion that they stop singing the song and stop all teasing and banter. I persuaded them to give it a go as a trial period and within three or four weeks every member of staff noticed a change in the whole atmosphere of the project. The biggest change was that children were much more likely to try new things and we were able to introduce a whole range of new play opportunities.

It never did me any harm

One final word on teasing. People often say to me, 'Well it never did me any harm'. I would reply to these people, 'It clearly has done you harm as you have *grown up with the need to undermine children to bolster your own self-worth'.* At least, this is what I would say if I was brave enough.

Teasing helpfulness?

I talked in Chapter 1 about a child on a rope swing. After that initial session Lorenzo actually helped me to load up the van at the end. His foster carer came to collect him, saw him helping out and said, *'Who is that child and what have you done with Lorenzo?'* So even when the child was exhibiting pro-social behaviour, he was being teased for this. If the foster carer thought he was being funny, he was wrong. If he thought that by teasing the child for positive behaviour he would somehow improve his behaviour, he was also wrong.

I have to praise him

So, the opposite of teasing would be praise, right? Well, not always. Working with extremely vulnerable children we find that sometimes a child's self-worth is so low that they automatically don't believe words of praise. They feel so worthless that they cannot believe the words of praise apply to them and consequently ignore them. This can have the additional negative effect of making the child distrust the adult because after all, if they have lied about that, what else have they lied about?

Now I don't want anyone to stop praising children after reading this. It is great to be praised and if you are a child that very rarely receives praise then it can be a wonderful moment of joy. What I am saying is for some children we need to do more.

Glorious

I worked with a head teacher of a special school recently delivering an inset day for his staff. He told me that the previous day a child with profound and multiple learning disabilities had been rushed to hospital due to serious health issues. The head teacher went with the child to be with him until his parents arrived. The head teacher could tell that the child was anxious, so he sat with him for over an hour playing very simple games. They took it in turns to touch each other's foreheads and then their noses. This simple act of being there for the child did more than any amount of praise. Interestingly the same head teacher was telling me about a child with extremely challenging behaviour. He described her as 'challenging but glorious!' It is no coincidence that a head teacher who repeatedly goes above and beyond for his children is also able to see even his more challenging children as 'glorious!'

That's nice dear

There is a very interesting bit of research by Stephen Grosz (Grosz, 2013; Popova, 2013) . He says that it is not the praise itself that is significant but the degree of presence and attentiveness we give to the child. Praise can be meaningless and empty, especially if it is insincere, and with vulnerable children this insincere praise can even be detrimental to children's self-worth. He argues that this kind of praise is more about the adults feeling they are doing the right thing than actually supporting confidence in children. However, what Grosz says is important is the presence and attentiveness we give to children on a daily basis. For some children, actively listening to them with interest is worth more than any words of praise because it shows them fundamentally that they are important to us. The 'presence' of just being there for the child while they play, showing by our body language and attitude that we are there if they need us can be more meaningful than words of praise. If we are being a calming and invested presence in what is really important for our children (play) then we are effectively 'praising' our children even if no words of praise are actually said. Even better we are supporting our most vulnerable children to feel worthwhile because whilst praise can simply fail to be believed our genuine interest in our children can instil feelings of self-worth by slipping in under the radar. This allows us to form a positive relationship with our children based on solid foundations of presence and attentiveness. An adult taking a genuine interest in a child and their world is really powerful. An adult playing with a child and validating their play can be even more powerful.

Parachute games

During our session the young boy who had such a heart-breaking experience of being teased by the outdoor pursuits leader became really interested in making bottle rockets (you can download bottle rocket instructions from my website www.inspiredchildren.org.uk (click on esources). I mentioned to him that we had once worked with an older children's group who had unsuccessfully attempted to fit parachutes to their rockets. This really intrigued the boy and so he spent the next twenty minutes making a parachute for his rocket. When it came time to launch, the whole group had stopped what they were doing to watch. On his first attempt he actually got the parachute to work and as the rocket floated gently to the ground, he received a thunderous round of applause from everyone watching.

Just comparing this experience to the one he had had at the outdoor pursuits centre we can see how profoundly important being surrounded by supportive adults rather than teasing ones can be for our children. It also shows just how amazing and special the child is as no one else has successfully made a working parachute.

What does this look like in practice?

Clearly if we want children to experience joy, we first need a solid platform of emotional safety. If we want a child to progress in any meaningful way, we must first and foremost ensure they feel fundamentally safe in our care. This can be a challenge because, as we will discuss later, sometimes the children that need us the most are the ones that struggle to be positive in their behaviour, attitude and language.

We also need to accept that when the child is experiencing any amygdala response from fear, anger or anxiety, every aspect of their learning and development is going to potentially be impaired. In addition to this they are significantly more likely to struggle with positive behaviour. We need, therefore, to have realistic expectations of our vulnerable children and try our best not to put unnecessary pressure on them because of this impairment. We need to accept that even simple everyday tasks may be a source of stress for our children. Even holding a pen is more difficult if your fingers have tensed up!

So, our first job is to help our children become calm and then provide an environment that is as free from anxiety as possible to help maintain that calm.

Attunement play

There are lots of ways in which we can reduce our amygdalae responses. In mammals, social experiences are key. Shared moments of laughter, soothing sounds and positive nurturing are absolutely vital tools for lowering our stress response. In fact, all of the aspects of joy we have explored are incredibly powerful at reducing the impact of the amygdala. Attunement play is particularly effective. Attunement play is shared play between a child and a carer. The actual play is less important than the shared joyful experience and any one-to-one games with a vulnerable child and an adult can be really effective. It could be peekaboo, pat-a-cake or word games, sensory play or singing songs together. It is the shared joyful experience which is important as these experiences are extremely powerful in calming down the amygdala and helping the child to come out of a dissociative state. For many of these games you need barely any resources and just a calming space to spend time with the child. Crucially this type of play may be something that is missing from their lives and so simply playing with a child in a calming environment, sharing moments of joy together could be the key to supporting their well-being.

In fact, pretty much all aspects of nurturing will help a child to calm their stress responses. Nurturing makes humans feel fundamentally safe and important. Just remember to tailor your nurturing to the child otherwise you may actually cause a stress response.

There are also physical ways in which we can calm our stress responses. Mindfulness can work really well for some children, and I have a wonderful mindfulness specialist on my team who has had some remarkable successes with children. The amazing children's artist and neurodiversity specialist Julia-Marie Harris (AKA JuliaArts https://juliaarts.co.uk) shared some really nice quick mindfulness tips with me when we last met. Because our fear response is to quicken our breathing, one way to 'trick' the amygdala into deactivating is simply to control our breathing. Taking short breaths in and longer breaths out, it has been suggested, can do just this. Julia suggested two short breaths in and a long breath out. This is something we can do quickly and easily with our children requiring no special resources. The best thing about this is it can give a child a tool they can use when they feel themselves getting stressed.

Remember we said at the beginning of this chapter that fear and anxiety make the muscles tense in expectation of fight or flight and our fingers tense up in preparation for punching things? Julia recommended firmly massaging the fingers below the knuckle. This relaxes our fingers which in turn 'tricks' the amygdala into deactivating. Again, we can do this together with a child, modelling tools they can use by themselves when needed. If the child trusts and feels safe with the adult this is even something we can do to each other, but you must be very sure of the relationship you have with the child and their previous experience of adults.

Mindfulness may not work for all children, but it is always worth a try

I personally struggle with mindfulness and in fact any activity that attempts to calm me. Whether this is something to do with my ADHD, my anxiety, or just stubbornness, but I automatically want to do the opposite of what people tell me to do and unfortunately this includes myself. Any attempt to consciously calm down will have the opposite result. However, the very evening after I met Julia I had a badminton match. I have a specific problem with badminton in that in a match situation I tense up and my serve becomes very erratic, either too high or straight into the net. My long-suffering partner has to put up with this every match and is pretty fed up. Did I mention that we lose, a lot? That evening I tried massaging my fingers in between each game and then two breaths in, one breath out, before every serve. I served so much better that we actually won a rare match. This does not mean I serve perfectly every time, I am still pretty bad at badminton after all, but it has made a significant improvement because it has just taken the edge off my anxiety.

It might be that these little techniques will work for some children but not for all children. Sometimes the trick is finding what does work. Observe the child at play, see where they feel the most comfortable. If that is during a certain type of play, then try to give as many opportunities as possible for that type of play. Try to find out what it is about that type of play that seems to calm or engage the child and try to replicate that with other play types. If the child is calmest with a particular worker, then try to expand that circle of social safety by playing alongside other workers at the same time. If the child is happiest in a particular environment, then try to ascertain what about that environment is calming and either seek to replicate it in less calming environments or even take elements from the safe environment with the child when they transition.

A chicken and egg conundrum

We know from early experiments with monkeys (Google Harlow's monkeys!) that exploratory behaviour is undermined when mammals do not feel safe. This means that the basic curiosity in children, which is a key motivator of all learning, is less apparent in vulnerable children as amygdala activation deactivates exploratory urges. However, we also know that sensory experiences are actually a good way to calm down stress responses. So, although the child will have less desire for sensory experiences, we know these experiences may well help them to alleviate their stress responses. So, without overloading the child's senses we can incrementally introduce sensory play and exploration, starting very small at first, and slowly increasing the levels of engagement as confidence grows and anxiety diminishes. We also know from working with children with a broad range of special needs that some children find strong sensory input to be extremely stressful and highly triggering. We therefore need to moderate the experiences to meet the needs of individual children.

For children who do not like loud noises, any setting with lots of children can be stressful. We can't and shouldn't make every child be quiet all the time. We do however need to provide certain times and places where the child can experience a quieter atmosphere.

Biting dinosaurs

We had a young child with very complex needs who really struggled with stress responses. His coping strategy was to bite himself so hard that he would draw blood. Now obviously this is a maladaptive strategy that is not at all good for the child. However, the one thing you should never do is force a child to stop using even

(Continued)

negative coping strategies without giving alternatives because no strategies at all can be even more damaging. We noticed that one of the few times the child felt calm was when he was playing with some large tactile dinosaurs. These particular dinosaurs are softer than the usual dinosaur toys but still 'realistic' enough to engage children. We managed to encourage the child to bite one of these dinosaurs instead of biting himself. This is still not a positive coping strategy, but it is a step in the right direction. This led to the child going to get a dinosaur from the cupboard whenever he felt stressed. This was the first time the child had taken control of his own stress and was beginning to manage his own mood. Eventually the child stopped biting the dinosaur altogether and began to hug and squeeze it instead. His previous self-harming behaviour almost completely stopped.

Brown trouser time

Another aspect of our stress response is that the amygdala does not operate in isolation. Our fear responses are based on several different criteria and so the amygdala needs information from other areas of our brain to determine whether to activate or not. Firstly, our fear response is dependent on our previous experiences and our memories of emotional events. Basically, the question is, *'has this happened before and was it brown trouser time?'*. This information comes from our hippocampus (amongst other areas of the brain for processing memory) and tells us if we need to be scared based on our memory of previous stressful or emotional events. We also need a situational awareness and context to assess the specific threat. Again, several areas of the brain come into play here, one being the pre-frontal cortex. So, if we see a lion, we are not scared, despite this being a dangerous predator, because our situational awareness tells us that we are in a zoo and that we are completely safe. Our previous memories of visiting zoos, where we were not attacked and eaten, reinforce this assessment of safety. Then we see the lion-sized hole in the bars of its cage and suddenly we are on full amygdala alert again.

Image 7.1 A lion eating someone by J

Some of you are already starting to see the problem here when working with children. The hippocampus is present from birth, but a young child will not have the memories needed to make an accurate assessment of threat. Also, the areas of the brain, such as the pre-frontal cortex, are still growing and developing, which mean they are less advanced than in adults and there is considerably less experience to draw upon. In short, the young child does not always accurately assess danger because the areas of the brain responsible for this are still works in progress and they simply don't have the necessary life experiences.

Does this mean that children are scared all the time? What it actually means is that children need to do something really rather clever if they are to accurately assess danger. Their hippocampus and pre-frontal cortex are clearly not up to the task, so they use the adults around them as a sounding board for danger. In effect, they outsource the job of assessing danger to the adults, effectively using our hippocampi and pre-frontal cortex to tell them what is safe and what is not. This is hugely significant for working with vulnerable children. Children will be arriving at our settings in a state of heightened threat response with all of the amygdala responses that entails. They do not know what is safe and what is dangerous because of the conflicting messages being given to them by adults.

A bearded man in the baby room?

I was delivering baby room training a couple of years ago and yet again there was a baby left over whose parents were late collecting him. (This seems a common occurrence in baby rooms!) The baby took one look at me and looked genuinely terrified. His amygdala had triggered so he was looking to his hippocampus to see if there were any emotional memories associated with men in the baby room. He'd never even seen a man in the baby room so he was drawing a blank. His amygdala was then looking to his pre-frontal cortex for an accurate assessment of the situation and coming back with a 'still under construction' message. With no additional information the baby would have remained in a state of fear. However, he happened to be sitting on his key worker's lap. He looked at her smiling face and relaxed body language as she chatted to me and then instantly turned to me and gave me a big beaming smile. He had used his key worker to accurately gauge the level of threat.

It is not just babies who outsource their threat assessment to the adults in their vicinity. Children do this all the way through childhood as a vital way in which they navigate the world. This means that as adults we need to be an accurate sounding board for danger for our children. We need to be telling children by our body language, tone of voice and behaviour that they are fundamentally safe. From the moment a child arrives in our setting they are synchronising their mood and behaviour with the adults around them and continuously assessing threat levels based on those same adults. If we are flustered, cross, mean sounding or anxious, our children will identify that there is clearly a threat, even if they can't see one, and their amygdalae will activate accordingly. If they see us behaving calmly, they will begin to feel safe even if they do identify a threat.

So, if a child sees a spider crawling across the nursery floor and the key worker screams and stamps on the spider in panic, the children will know that there is a threat and their anxiety levels will sky rocket. If the key worker smiles, sings, 'Incy Wincy Spider', and then ushers the spider outside with a glass and a bit of paper, the children will know they are safe and maybe even become fascinated with the spider and other bugs.

Image 7.2   A person screaming when they see a spider by R

The school run from hell!

As parents we've all had that school or nursery run where everything goes wrong. 'Where are you shoes? Where is your bag? Why have you suddenly taken all your clothes off? And now the dog's been sick!' We are late, flustered and the traffic is a nightmare. Obviously, we are stressed and understandably so. Our children will begin to synchronise their mood with ours and consequently their amygdala triggers causing the accompanying stress responses. We then drop them off at school and nursery where their heightened threat response is now someone else's problem. So, if we actually work in a nursery or school we could have children arriving at our setting on full amygdala alert merely because their parents got stuck for ages at the temporary purple lights at the top of Coventry Road. The children have not had an accurate sounding board to assess threat and so are struggling to feel safe. This will impact on their behaviour and their capacity to learn. From the second they arrive at our setting they need to know that they are OK.

Meltdown

And what happens if the child loses control? The tantrum, the meltdown, rage or seeing red? They are effectively incapable of learning in this state. No amount of behaviour techniques is going to make any difference to that child. What is needed more than anything is a supportive adult to help them manage the crisis they are experiencing. The last thing they need is cross adults punishing them because all this does is prolong the crisis.

Many of us have experienced fear and even rage before. We might have an argument with our partner for instance and become so angry we lose the ability to speak. This is because communication and language are upper brain functions that can be effectively disconnected in the throes of anger.

If this happens to a child, a well-meaning adult may well say to the child, 'Use your words'. This is not helpful. If the child could use their words they would. Imagine if, in the middle of the aforementioned argument with your partner, your partner said to you, 'Use your words!' I am guessing that would not have helped you calm down and would have probably had the opposite effect.

Not what I meant at all!

During one training session for midday supervisors, I suggested to the team that instead of constantly treating extremely minor injuries with a cold compress, they should gently encourage the children to carry on playing, because that way they would produce all of the lovely pain relief biochemicals and would soon forget about their injury. The next session one midday supervisor said, 'You'll be proud of me because I did what you said last week. A child came up to me because they had hurt themselves and I said, "You're confusing me with someone who cares!"' This is not what I meant at all!

It may be unavoidable that there are going to be mean adults in children's lives. We can help protect children from these adults by being positive, supportive and nurturing. We cannot protect them by being mean too. All teasing and banter do for children is to reinforce a child's world view of adults as a source of fear and humiliation. Even if you truly believe such behaviour is harmless, please try to find a different way. There are so many wonderful things you have the power to be for your children so why would we choose to be someone who ridicules and teases. I also believe that sometimes we need to stand up to the adults who treat children with contempt. We need to challenge them and question them because if we don't speak out then it is a sure thing that the children will not have the confidence or power to do so.

Teased if you do, teased if you don't!

You may find yourselves working with groups of children who experience a lot of teasing even from family members. It is more important than ever that you show an alternative approach. Show children that, at least when they are with you, they are safe, respected and important. On one inner city project I noticed that parents were teasing their own children mercilessly if the child got something wrong or failed at something. What was even more heart-breaking was that the children were also teased if they did something well or showed any signs of intelligence. They were teased if they used long words or teased if they did well on a test at school. We are now talking about children who are growing up to see success at learning as something to be disparaged and ridiculed. This is catastrophic for a child's cultural capital and their social aspirations. It also puts a child in the dismal position of not being able to do anything without negative responses and pretty much ensuring their behaviour deteriorates.

Also, let's always remember that the presence and attentiveness we give to children is profoundly important. The amazing Jo Stockdale from Well Within Reach (https://wellwithinreach.co.uk) delivers insightful training and writes some amazing articles about how we can truly understand children's behaviour and address their needs. She is well worth looking up as she is incredibly passionate about improving outcomes for children. Just spend some time with your children, support them to play and show genuine interest in what interests them. Shared moments of joy between the child and the adult change lives.

Our own mental health is key

Sometimes the most important thing we need to do to help bring joy back to our children is to recognise when we ourselves are struggling. We need to be open and honest about our mental health and help each other when things are tough. Remember that we can sometimes feel as if everything we do is in the face of an overwhelming gale force wind. A study by the Early Years Alliance showed that mental health among early years workers is critically low (Early Years Alliance, 2018). Working with children is underpaid, undervalued and emotionally exhausting, which can make for challenging days even if your mental health is good. If you are struggling with your mental health, then it is beyond exhausting. It is very easy to feel alone when you are struggling with mental health issues but there are many, many people who are struggling too. If we realise this and begin to support each other, we might just improve outcomes for our children. I delivered an online training course recently about working with refugee children. During part of the course I did something I had never done before. Whilst talking about the effects of anxiety, I actually admitted I was currently taking anxiety medication. The reason I had never done this was simple embarrassment, as if my anxiety was somehow something to be ashamed of. Within a few seconds, three other people on the course wrote in the group chat that they were also taking medication for anxiety. I found this incredibly comforting and moving. Perhaps we sometimes need to remind ourselves that we work in one of the most caring sectors in the world and we need to care for each other as well as our children.

Home from home

It is also vitally important that we try to create a home from home in our settings. The feeling of safety and well-being this can achieve is profound and life changing. Try to imagine what your setting feels like to a child and try to find ways to make it the safest, most nurturing space you can.

Snuggle time

I visited a special school recently and, in each classroom, they had a giant four poster bed so that the teacher could read bedtime stories with all of the children snuggled up and comfortable. Also ideal for teachers needing an afternoon nap!

A final thought

OK, so a thought occurred to me recently. If we accept that shared social experiences calm down our threat response and help children who are beginning to dissociate, and we also accept that calming breathing is important for calming children, then there just happens to be a ready-made experience that can be utterly amazing for our children. Something we do almost every day that automatically makes us take a shorter breath in and a longer breath out. Something that gives us joy and makes us smile.

Yes, I'm talking once again about singing. Singing will almost always entail a shorter breath in and then a longer breath out as we hold certain notes.

This means that singing has mindfulness built in! Singing has a unique capacity to lift our mood so let's all sing more with our children!

Summary

So, we have learnt that a lack of joy is catastrophic for our children and if we want to make any progress we need to support them to feel safe, important and nurtured at all times. We know that when the amygdala activates children can really struggle and so calming them should be our first priority. We now know who stole our joy. Clowns - clowns stole our joy! We also need to be open about mental health, supportive of our colleagues and, above all, sing!

8

WE ARE CELESTIAL – BEING A DIFFERENT SORT OF GROWN-UP

Not all vulnerable children are quiet

It would be a comforting conceit that our most vulnerable children are all quiet, withdrawn children who just need loving and nurturing to help them thrive. Indeed, I work with many children for who this is exactly the case. Their life experiences have caused them to dissociate with the world and withdraw into themselves and the most powerful thing for these children is to have loving nurturing adults in their lives.

However, some of our loudest, cockiest, least well-behaved and, if we're honest, least likeable children are also incredibly vulnerable. They are fundamentally unable to behave positively because there has been a profound lack of positive experiences in their life. These children may need joy more than any other child.

As adults who work with children, we have a simple choice when confronted with a child who is aggressive, frustrated and does not know how to use positive language or behaviour. We can meet the child's aggression with more aggression, sanctions and negativity or we can see through the behaviour to the child underneath and give that child a different role model.

Seeing through behaviour

I had a life changing experience many years ago when visiting my mum in hospital who was extremely ill with cancer. I walked into the ward and there was a man in the bed opposite who was shouting obscenities and kicking and punching whilst six members of hospital staff attempted to hold him down. He was a huge man with unkempt hair, tattoos and matted beard. I just kept my head down and walked past without making eye contact. The next day I visited my mum again and was appalled to find her sitting on the end of his bed chatting with this man. I am not proud of this but when he was out of earshot, I actually told my mum off for talking to the man saying, 'Why would you want to talk to such a horrible man?' I will never forget her reply. She said, 'Oh, he was just scared, he'd had a heart attack and it was the worst day of his life. He's quite a nice bloke really!' The sad thing is that no one else had this viewpoint. The doctors and nurses all treated him with hostility after his violent episode. Now I am not excusing his behaviour, and I fully understand why a medical professional who had been sworn at and punched the previous day would not want to be kind in return. The truth is that only one person in that ward saw through the huge, bearded man to the frightened little boy that he was underneath and that was my mum. Even whilst extremely ill herself she helped this man through the most difficult time in his life.

I realised then that there were children who I did not give my full attention to because their behaviour was challenging or their language negative or for any number of other reasons. In short, I was judging children purely by their behaviour and never looking deep enough to help the child underneath. However, this one simple gift my mum gave me taught me I have to be better than this. I have to give the same amount of care, attention and nurturing to a child who behaves negatively towards me that I would to a child who treats me positively. I have to realise that much of the aggression and frustration exhibited by a child is not personal, not aimed at me, but more likely a reaction to the negativity and fear in their world.

Redressing the balance in children's lives

I believe in a very simple equation for working with vulnerable children. If a child has a higher percentage of positive experiences in their life than negative, they are much more likely to thrive. If, however, a child has more negative than positive experiences then they are much more likely to struggle. The good news about this is that I don't believe it is based on the amount of time spent with a child but on the quality of interactions. You may only spend a couple of hours with a child but if you make that time nurturing, joyful and amazing you can have a profound impact. If you work in after-school clubs this is exactly the situation you will find yourself in, potentially having only two hours of time to overcome a child's negative experiences of life. I believe my role in working with vulnerable children is to provide such incredibly positive experiences that it helps to offset the negative experiences that have been so damaging for them.

This is why the concept of joy is so important. Joyful experiences are more potent than the normal experiences of life and are consequently much more effective at offsetting negativity in a child's life.

Bless you

A child once sneezed directly into my face. He then dutifully put his hand over his mouth as he had been told by an adult that he should put his hand over his mouth when he sneezed. He looked genuinely pleased with himself that he had remembered this simple courtesy. I thought, 'So near and yet so far', as the snot slowly dripped down my glasses.

Let's be a little more forgiving

We also need to realise that all of those lovely upper brain functions such as empathy, moral code and social behaviours are the last bits of our brains to mature, potentially not until 25 years old. This means that 4-year-olds have a long way to go and we should not be so hard on them when they make mistakes. Just as we are supportive of our children when they make mistakes in communicating, we should also be supportive when their young brains make mistakes in terms of behaviour.

A fake smile

I was working with reception class children recently and a group of young boys had excluded another boy, making him upset. In my most reasonable voice I explained the situation to the boys and then without thinking asked, 'How would you feel if someone left you out of a game?' The young boys all in unison said, 'Sad!' whilst beaming huge grins at me. Had I unlocked the empathy in their young brains? Of course not. They were just telling me what they thought I wanted to hear.

This does not mean that children can't show empathy, it simply means that it is a work in progress, and they are at the start of a very long journey. We should be a little more forgiving of our children's behaviour because they are still developing.

Getting away with it

There is also a myth that if we don't meet negative behaviour with negative consequences, we are somehow letting the child get away with it. This is not the case. By dealing with behaviour positively and scaffolding and supporting pro-social choices we are giving children the ability to make positive choices in the future and steering them to more positive behaviour. If we work with children, it is never in our remit to make children feel rubbish. Surely, supporting children to behave positively in the future is a more important goal than keeping an imaginary score of whether a child has felt suitably bad enough for each individual instance of behaviour?

Finger in the ear

Whilst waiting outside my daughter's drama lesson I saw a little boy jumping on and off a wall shouting, 'Daddy, look at me!' His father stared resolutely at his phone and ignored him. Eventually the little boy walked along the wall and stuck his finger in his dad's ear. The dad then shouted at his son in anger.

I recently met Sandi Phoenix at the Childcare & Education Expo. Sandy is a childcare and behaviour specialist whose take on behaviour is absolutely fascinating and well worth looking into further. She proposes alternatives to behaviourism approaches (reward and consequence) based on up-to-date psychology and a solid understanding of children's well-being (Phoenix, 2021). She looks at children's fundamental needs and how practitioners can ensure their children's well-being and pro-social behaviour by supporting children to fulfil their needs. Best of all she mentions joy!

Queen for the day

On our adoption activity days, we always brief the adopters before the session starts. One thing we tell them is that they don't have to wait for the children to start playing to play themselves. As a way of calming their nerves or just for fun, they are always welcome to come and make a den or magic potions with us, even if there are no children present at the time. One benefit of this is that it gives potential adopters ideas to use with their children when they do adopt. Another benefit is the idea that, if you build it, they will come! Often if the adults start playing, the children will now see playful adults rather than adults standing around, and are much more likely to join in. In short, adults expressing joy in play inspires the children to join in too. On one event a group of adopters got together to build a giant castle out of cardboard boxes. No children joined in until the very last tower was finished when, seemingly out of nowhere, a little girl with Down's syndrome appeared in the castle. She was wearing a full queen costume complete with crown, and it seemed like the most natural thing in the world for her to take ownership of the castle that her toiling minions had made for her. The joy she experienced in her very own castle made every bit of effort worth it!

Children do what works

If you really want to understand the concept of behaviour, then the simplest way of looking at it is that children do what works. A child is not behaving without purpose and every behaviour exhibited is in response to a need. Children do whatever works in each given situation to achieve that need regardless of whether that behaviour is considered positive or negative by the adults around them. Case in point is the little boy who stuck his finger in his dad's ear. The positive expressions of behaviour, 'Look at me, Daddy' were being ignored so because these behaviours were not working to fulfil the boy's need for connection, he escalated his behaviour to something that would work. Namely, plopping his finger in his dad's ear. This is also a classic example of a play cue, which we explored in my first book.

This means that if a child has never had positive methods of coping modelled for them, they are almost always going to default to a negative strategy because that is the only way they know that works. If, however, a positive behaviour pattern supports the child to experience joy then the child is much more likely to default to the pro-social behaviour because now the child has options.

This means that modelling positive behaviour is even more important for our children because without it children can become stuck in a loop of negativity with no positive strategies to draw upon.

Never dismiss attention

This brings us onto attention. One of my colleagues at Inspired Children is a wonderful person called Diana Lawton. She is our resident specialist in behaviour, attachment, self-regulation, neurodiversity and just being special. Diana becomes extremely frustrated by people who dismiss attention seeking behaviours in children. The familiar attitude of, '*Oh he's just attention seeking, ignore him*' fills Diana with a genuine rage. The simple reason is that if we dismiss this behaviour and ignore it, we are basically ignoring all of the feelings of disempowerment that have led to these behaviours. No child ever gets up in the morning and decides to 'seek some attention'. These behaviours come from a desire to feel important and quite often feeling the opposite. So, if a child exhibits 'attention seeking behaviours' they are most likely struggling with disempowerment and needing to feel important and worthwhile. By ignoring and dismissing these behaviours we are in essence telling the child that they are utterly unimportant to us, thus re-enforcing the very feelings that have led to the behaviour in the first place.

Sandi Phoenix echoes Diana's views and says that so-called 'attention seeking behaviours' should be described as seeking 'connection'. I really like this. It turns something that is often dismissed and even treated with derision into a vital social function.

It wasn't me!

So sometimes a child will do what works in a given situation only to find it doesn't work. Without alternatives they can easily get stuck in the behaviour pattern despite it being ineffective. A classic example is a child you have watched do something and who then denies it to your face even though they know you have seen them do it. So, let's imagine Abidemi has stolen the red paint. You watched him steal the paint, he is still holding the red paint and his hands are covered in red paint (literally red-handed). In addition, you have four separate eyewitness statements, CCTV footage of him stealing the paint and CSI Miami have positive DNA samples confirming his guilt. And what does Abidemi say? *'It wasn't me'*. But you caught him on camera!

Now this particular behaviour makes us very cross. It appears to show a disrespect to the adult and so we become much more aggressive to the child attempting to force them into admitting they stole the paint. Yet still Abidemi denies it. There then follows a battle of wills between the adult and the child and still Abidemi denies it. In some cases, the only way you are going to get Abidemi to admit his guilt is if you fundamentally break his spirit by escalating the level of punishments until they are entirely disproportionate to the very minor offence of taking the red paint. This is an extremely negative experience for all concerned (just ask Shaggy).

The truth is that Abidemi is not being disrespectful, he just doesn't want you to be mean to him. He dislikes being told off, and who doesn't. Previously he might have successfully used the *'It wasn't me'* defence and it did work to avoid the negative experience of being told off. So, Abidemi is doing what works to avoid that negative experience except in this case it isn't working. This does not mean he can automatically come up with another strategy whilst being shouted at and so he becomes stuck with a failing strategy but with no recourse but to stick with it because his growing brain, which is now under increased stress, cannot find an alternative.

So, this is an interesting way of looking at it. The only reason Abidemi has lied in the first place is because he is, understandably, trying to avoid the negative experience of being reprimanded. So, who is responsible for this behaviour? We, the adults who have made the child fear our response, or the child who is very sensibly trying to avoid feeling negative? Not only do we sometimes create negative behaviour in our children we also reward it by the very methods we use to attempt to curb the behaviour. If a child is seeking connection by exhibiting negative behaviour because this is the only strategy they know how to use, then any amount of shouting or telling off is still a connection of sorts and so the child is now being rewarded for their behaviour.

I suppose then, we should amend the earlier statement about behaviour to: children do what works, even when it doesn't. This pretty much holds true with every age of child and does give us one of the most useful methods for steering children towards positive behaviour. It also highlights the crucial role of joy in supporting behaviour.

Approaches to behaviour based on joy

Here is how we look at behaviour. If a child is exhibiting a behaviour that could be seen as negative, we try to ascertain why this behaviour is working for the child and what feelings or needs the child is trying to avoid or experience. We then give the child the same feelings or connection through positive and joyful

experiences. If a child experiences joy through the positive behaviours, addressing the need or feeling that has led to the negative behaviour, then they not
only learn alternatives but produce addictive biochemicals which make them
feel amazing. This means the child is much more likely to choose the pro-social
behaviours because they work equally well, if not better, to address their needs
and they crave the positive feelings associated with the behaviour.

So, if the child is seeking connection but does not have positive methods for
doing this, they are likely to exhibit negative behaviour just to overcome the
feelings of disempowerment and to gain some form of connection. So instead,
we give the children positive connections through our presence and attentiveness, we reinforce the child's self-worth by spending time with them and we
make sure the child has alternative approaches modelled by the adults around
them.

Now there are no miracle cures for behaviour, especially if you work with
some of the more vulnerable children. However, this simple method has worked
for many of our children and to have a whole staff team using this approach
has been utterly transformative.

Spilled juice

I heard an absolutely fantastic example of behaviour from a neurodiversity
specialist. Unfortunately, this was a long time ago and so I have completely forgotten the name of the specialist, so if this sounds familiar to anyone, please
get in touch so I can credit the person responsible.

A little boy in a nursery would repeatedly spill his drink at snack time. He
was told off, made to clean up, and then made to sit in a corner by himself for
the remainder of snack time. His parents were contacted but they were baffled
as he never exhibited this behaviour at home.

So, the first job is to try to work out why this behaviour is working for the
child. For what reasons might a child repeatedly spill his drink and what feelings and motivations are involved in his behaviour?

There could be several possible answers, so the first job is to narrow that
down. This can be done from observations of the child, discussions with key
workers or other adults or even trial and error. It might be that the child is
simply seeking connection and so the very telling off is giving him what he
needs in that moment. He might hate the taste of the juice and so he is, sensibly, avoiding a negative experience by spilling the drink. He might love the way
the drink swirls as it spills and is engaging his curiosity system, the rewards
for which we now know are intense and powerful. He might not like blue cups.
In any of these circumstances the inevitable telling off is either rewarding the
behaviour and ensuring its continuation or is not a sufficient deterrent to overcome the stimulation the child is receiving from the behaviour.

So why did the child spill the drink? Well, the neurodiversity specialist in question observed the child at snack time and within ten minutes knew exactly why the child was spilling his drink. He loved cleaning up. So, none of the telling off and unpleasantness was in any way going to stop the behaviour because the child was being rewarded with the very thing he craved. All the neurodiversity specialist had to do was suggest that if the child did not spill his drink he could use the big broom afterwards to help sweep up. The child never spilt his drink again. By replacing the negative behaviour with a joyful alternative, the child had everything he needed to make pro-social choices and ultimately to have a more rewarding time in the nursery because he was getting the feelings he craved without the accompanying negative emotions.

Well, she was terrible wasn't she!

I worked with a child called Jack who had extremely challenging behaviour from day one. It soon became very clear that the reason for his behaviour was that he felt utterly worthless. Because Jack felt that he could not do anything well, what worked for him was to stop other children being successful. So, for instance, Jack believed he could not play football well so he would run onto a football pitch and boot the ball over a fence before running away laughing. Jack believed he could not draw or paint well so he would grab someone else's artwork and rip it up before running away laughing. This pattern of behaviour was extremely disruptive, and the sanctions placed upon him by his school only reinforced the behaviour patterns. The reason for his behaviour was pretty clear in that Jack's parents were openly disparaging of him and treated him with aggressive contempt. He was constantly in trouble both at school and with the police. Basically, Jack felt so utterly worthless that his only recourse was to make other people feel undervalued. The closest Jack ever came to experiencing joy was when he was destroying someone else's ability to experience joy. As you can imagine, this behaviour is one of the most challenging to combat. All we could do is to make sure that at our after-school project Jack felt important and experienced moments of joy from positive actions rather than from hurting others. We made sure we created an oasis of calm for Jack and treated him like a valued member of the group. One thing that really helped was getting Jack to film a documentary of the project. He took to the task with absolute dedication because he suddenly felt like the most important person on the whole project. In no other area of his life would he have been trusted with an expensive video camera.

The turning point for Jack came when he sat down next to me on a step. This in itself was something quite rare and special. He then said to me, 'I've had a sh*t day at school'. I knew in that moment that this was most likely the first time in

(Continued)

his life he had felt safe enough to talk about his day with an adult. He then told me about his extremely challenging day (he was right, it was sh*t). There are no quick fixes for children with self-esteem this low. Working with Jack was an uphill battle in the face of almost overwhelming negativity but over the months he began to show incredible progress. So much so, that we invited him to join a focus group for the entire region to help steer the project. He proved himself to be incredibly incisive and a genuine asset to the group. He even sat on job interview panels for prospective applicants for working on the project. He was absolutely brilliant, and we only had to challenge him once in the whole time he did the job. After one job interview, he said, 'Well, she was terrible wasn't she!' and all we had to remind him of was, 'Just wait till she leaves the room next time!'

Ten naughty monkeys jumping on the bed

Older readers may remember the adverts for PG Tips tea which featured fully clothed chimpanzees sitting at tables whilst delicately sipping tea from china teacups. This was not achieved with CGI but using real chimps from a zoo in the Midlands called Twycross Zoo. Now if you have ever visited Twycross Zoo you will know that these chimps are not sitting delicately sipping tea. The chimps are arguably the most terrifying creatures in the whole zoo.

My mum was a teacher and often went on school trips to Twycross Zoo. During one such trip, a chimp, in what can only be described as horrendous stereotyping, threw a banana at a child which bounced harmlessly off the bars (the banana not the child). Now remember that chimpanzees have incredible problem-solving brains, so the ape decided that if hard objects are going to bounce it needed to throw something softer. You can guess the rest: my mum spent half an hour wiping ape poo out of a very upset child's eye.

This is a long way from the gentle, tea sipping creatures from the adverts. The weird thing was that my mum said the chimpanzee, 'laughed' when it happened. I have since witnessed this behaviour myself. At a recent visit, a bird got into the chimpanzee enclosure. The noise was incredible as the chimpanzees hunted the bird down and killed it. I can only describe the sound they made as joy. It was a terrifying and primal joy but joy none-the-less and it was deeply upsetting to watch. So, what is this joy that revels in death, this animal expression of the darkest of natures?

I believe this is the other side of the coin that I have been describing throughout this book. I believe there is a darker side to joy, not just in chimpanzees but in humans. There are human beings who revel in other's pain, who laugh at genuine misfortune and who enjoy cruelty, humiliation and hurting other people. I believe this dark side of joy is the enemy of everything it means to be an enlightened and caring society.

I mentioned in my first book about working in young offenders' institutions with young men who were dads. We were helping them to be able to be positive parents for their children when they finished their sentences. During the project we discussed the young men's own childhood experiences. Not a single one had anything positive to say about their own fathers. In every single case their dads had been abusive and violent. One of the best outcomes from this project was that a majority of the young men became determined to not be like their dads and to be better role models for their children than the ones they had experienced growing up.

I believe the answer to this dark side of joy is to re-engage the child with the positive sides of joy. This means that an early years setting full of joy, laughter, awe and wonder is giving the child something very unique and potentially supporting the child to become a pro-social human being. Once again, I believe awe and wonder are crucially important. I have no evidence to base this on, but I don't believe that aggressive people, who only show joy in violence and cruelty, can appreciate awe, wonder or beauty in the same way. I don't think they see the amazingness in the world because they have been conditioned not to. I therefore believe that if we give a child a fundamental joy in the world then this is the most powerful antidote to the darker joy of cruelty and violence. If we show children the incredible joy in the natural world, a sunset or clouds, trees, animals, stars and planets, undersea creatures or rocks and fossils then I believe this is the best defence against cruelty. And what about music, art, dancing, poetry or singing or in fact any of the amazing things in the world? If we show children joy in these things then I believe we are helping our children to choose positive joy over cruelty.

A profound difference

About seven years ago I saw two young boys during school lunchtime, lying down and looking at clouds. The midday supervisor approached them and shouted, 'Get up off the floor, you'll get filthy. Go and play over there'. About six months ago the exact same thing happened. It was a different school in a different county, but two young boys were lying down looking at clouds. The midday supervisor approached them, lay down next to them and chatted about clouds before moving on.

This is what I am talking about. A simple choice to be the adult who supports joy or the adult who takes it away. I don't think that the second midday supervisor even realised how amazing she was, but I believe what she did was profoundly important not just for the two young boys but maybe for our society as a whole.

Just say squeak

OK, a really bizarre bit of research is the 'Rat Park' studies in the late 1970's (Hadaway et al., 1979). Basically, two groups of rats were offered a choice between morphine solution in their feeding bottles or just water. One group of rats had been raised in a sterile cage environment whilst the other group were raised in 'Rat Park' which was a huge purpose-built environment where they had lots more space and loads of things to do. The study showed that the rats who grew up in the more stimulating environment did not ingest as much morphine and the study was subsequently used as a parallel to housing issues leading to drug addiction in humans. Basically, rats that live in a more positive environment are less likely to turn to drugs. A joyful experience of life is the antidote to self-destructive behaviours!

What this study is saying is that if we experience a positive environment, we are much more likely to make pro-social choices. Basically, joyful experiences lead us to make better choices.

Now obviously, things with humans are not as simple as this and many more factors are involved in human addiction. There have been subsequent studies that back up the Rat Park findings but there are also others that do not and so the study does have its detractors.

I think maybe the detractors are missing something important here. The scientists built a rat park, an actual park for rats! Some wonderful, weird and very special human beings spent days of their time and probably large sums of money making a rat park. Please let there have been rat swings and rat roundabouts and especially a rat see-saw! There certainly is in my imagination. No other species on the planet comes close to the weird and wonderful ideas that humans have. Only a species that understands the joy of exploring and experimenting can come up with the idea of building a park for rats. So maybe it doesn't prove conclusively that a positive environment can support pro-social behaviours (although it is highly suggestive of this) but it does prove what a simple joy of science can lead to, with a lot of imagination and a decent research grant. The only shame is that they never got a chance to move on the phase two, 'Rat Theme Park'. The cost of the rat rollercoasters and rat waltzers was not within budget so we can only imagine the fun those rats would have had.

Image 8.1   Rats playing on a see-saw by K

What does this look like in practice

One thing writing this book has taught me is that children get everything from the adults around them. They model everything about their behaviour, their attitude to life, their social responses, their mood and even how they cope in stressful situations. It is very rare that children can choose the adults around them. Children are therefore completely powerless in terms of the behaviours and attitude of the adults in their environment. But we are not.

We have the power to choose to be any role model we want for our children. This is incredibly important. In a world where we can choose exactly what type of role model we are for our children, let's choose joy. We could choose to be just one more adult, reinforcing negative cycles of fear and aggression, or we can be better.

If we acknowledge that some children do not have positive influences on their lives and that this will fundamentally impact on their behaviour, then we can choose to be a different sort of grown-up.

This is important for all of our children but especially important for our more vulnerable children. If a child has overwhelmingly negative experiences of adults, they are likely to view all adults with suspicion and fear. This means that merely by being an adult we are automatically a source of fear to some children. The only way we are going to be able to support those children to thrive is if we challenge their preconceptions of adults. I mentioned this in my first book but I want to take it a step further. Every vulnerable child we work with must come to a fundamental realisation about us. *'She's not like other grown-ups'*, or *'He's not like other grown-ups'*. This simple thought process is the gateway to well-being because once the child has begun this process the very next question is, *'Can I trust this grown-up?'* And once the answer is emphatically, 'YES!' then we can begin to support the child to heal.

Jack, who finally felt comfortable enough to actually sit next to an adult and talk about his problems had begun to understand that we were not like the other adults in his life, and we were there for him. The presence and attentiveness we gave him showed Jack that we had his back, both emotionally and physically, and this simple truth was utterly transformative.

The power of joy once removed

So, I have already mentioned that on our adoption activity days we tell adopters to play even when there are no children present because this will inspire children to join in. Well on one session a couple decided to use our foam bricks to make a dinosaur cave. At first no children joined in and the two men continued to play happily by themselves. After twenty minutes, during which they thoroughly enjoyed making their dinosaur cave, a young boy approached them holding a dinosaur and said, 'Can he play too?' The two adopters then spent an amazing twenty minutes building the most incredible dinosaur cave with the little boy. The joy they shared led to an expression of interest, which started the adoption process for that little boy, which hopefully will lead to a forever family.

The story does not end there though; there is another layer of joy that occurred much later. The bricks the adopters used had been kindly donated by TTS who make all sorts of resources for working with children. I told the fantastic Michelle, who is my contact at TTS, all about the wonderful joy the bricks had inspired. Michelle then contacted the lady who had designed the bricks and told her of the impact they had had on the adoption activity day. Apparently, the designer of the bricks had tears in her eyes as she learned just how profound the experience had been for the little boy.

So, this is joy that has been passed on, second hand joy if you will, but still with the power to move us to tears.

How do children know we are different?

So how do we show a child at the deepest of levels that we are not like other grown-ups? In my first book I suggested that being playful and fun are a vital way we show this to our children. The two men playing with dinosaurs showed the child they were not like other grown-ups because they were sitting on the floor playing. However, this is not the only way in which we can show our children we are different. It is not just the outgoing, larger than life adults that can engage our most vulnerable children. It is fantastic to have these playful adults on your team, but our children all have different personalities and ways of expressing themselves and so do the adults. Simply listening to a child shows you are a different sort of grown-up. Giving the child responsibility when no one else would, giving them choices, and being there for them when they need you the most all show the child that not only are they important to you, but you are a different sort of grown-up. If you take an interest in what interests the child, no matter how childish it might seem, then you validate the child's interests and become a partner to share joy with.

In a world where we can be any role model we choose, let's choose to be the different sort of adult who gives joy instead of taking it away. Let's be the mid-day supervisor who lies down next to children and chats about clouds rather than the one who limits and belittles a child's joy.

We need to see through children's behaviour to the child underneath and understand their feelings and needs. Remember the road to empathy begins with 'how would I feel if?' and so we need to demonstrate our own empathy by understanding how the world feels to our children.

We need to understand that children's behaviour is rarely personal. Verbal and even physical attacks on us when a child is in a full blown crisis are not specifically aimed at us but merely because we happen to be there at that moment. We can match their aggression with more aggression, or we can understand that in that instance they need nurturing and supporting. When training my own staff, I describe it as the '*Cliff of calm*'. The children may crash against us like an angry sea, but we remain calm. Only then can we begin to support the child toward pro-social behaviour and well-being. We also need to understand that a child who is in crisis does not need behaviour strategies based on negative reinforcement. They need an adult who has their back and can help them when they are struggling.

The incredible autism advocate John Simpson talks about his experiences of growing up with autism and is utterly inspiring to listen to. He says that some days he can make choices and other days this causes him anxiety. Sometimes the best thing to do is make choices for him but obviously not every day. He, like all of our children, needs people who understand him and can respond in a way that is appropriate to his needs on a day-by-day basis. This has made me consider my own practice (and as a parent). I have always believed that giving children choice is empowering and extremely beneficial for children. Of course, this is often the case, but it seems not always.

Working on camps with children with school anxiety I have noticed they sometimes struggle to make simple choices such as '*What do you want for lunch?*' Previously I have persisted in trying to pin the child down for a response as it can be exasperating not knowing what to cook for children and I desper-ately want to empower them by giving them a choice (whether they want it or not!). Now I know that sometimes they need someone to just say, '*I've made you a huge pile of scrambled eggs, tuck in!*'

Made of stars?

One more amazing thing I learnt whilst researching the astronomy training: our own sun is quite small (comparatively) and only produces helium. It will never produce more complex elements like carbon or iron. Yet the earth and even our own bodies are full of complex elements. So where did they come from if not produced by our own sun? The only place these elements are produced is in giant stars like Betelgeuse. This means that every atom and molecule in our bodies was actually produced in a giant star billions of miles away that exploded millions of years ago. So, we are all literally made of stars. Every child in your setting is a celestial being because all of the atoms in their bodies were once part of a giant star.

Joy vs cruelty

This bit is really important. I believe that the more we experience joy in the world the less we will seek joy through negative means. I believe you have to be able to see the beauty in the world to want to preserve it and I believe our ability to see awe and wonder, to experience joy in the everyday beauty of the world is the direct opposite of the joy of hurting and humiliating. In short, I don't think chimpanzees can appreciate a beautiful sunset.

I honestly believe that if we give our children joy through uniquely human experiences, they are more likely to grow up to be pro-social human beings. If we show our children joy in art, music, poetry, dancing or even a well-crafted maths problem then they will be more likely to resist their inner chimpanzee when they are older. I believe that we need to stop and experience the joy of a beautiful sunrise, ice patterns on a car window and the shapes of the clouds if we want our children to grow up with that same joy inside them.

And the best hairstyle award goes to the alpaca!

Nurturing and caring for animals has proven to be extremely therapeutic for vulnerable children and there are lots of animal therapy centres across the UK. I saw this first hand when we took our vulnerable children on an alpaca walk and saw the absolute joy and delight at being with these wonderful (and very fluffy) animals. I have since worked in a special school where they actually have alpacas in the outdoor area. I think this is another factor that can be the antidote to cruelty: the simple joy of companionship with animals.

I realise we have gone far beyond current research here but one thing that is absolutely certain is that you cannot do any harm to your children by inspiring joy in the world. Whilst many of the behaviour 'management' strategies still used by education establishments have been proved to be at best ineffective and at worst damaging for children, the pursuit of joyful experiences cannot only support pro-social behaviour but will in no way harm children. Judy Willis says that not one single neuroimaging or neurochemistry experiment has ever shown that a joyful approach will harm a child (Willis, 2007). And always remember that joyful experiences produce corresponding biochemicals, some of which are addictive. Children will crave these joyful experiences meaning they are less likely to seek negative experiences.

Summary

So, this alternatively light and dark chapter has shown us that we need to see through behaviour to the child underneath. We learned that negative environments, with joy absent, are almost guaranteed to create negative behaviour in our children because joy is the key motivator for pro-social behaviour. We also learned that we need to be a different kind of grown-up and inspiring joy in the world is the best antidote for cruelty. We all need to find joy in the world and pass this joy on to our children.

    We learned that rats love see-saws, astronomy is cool, and if we dismiss attention seeking as merely negative behaviour without understanding the motivations behind the behaviour then Diana Lawton will come round our houses and throw rocks through our windows (or maybe cake). We also learned that we are all made of stars. We are literally celestial.

9

SIMPLE EQUATIONS FOR THRIVING – HOW JOY CAN CHANGE NOT JUST CHILDREN BUT OUR ENTIRE SOCIETY

When I started this book, I was frustrated because I could see something tangible and powerful transforming the lives of vulnerable children, but it seemed like no one else had noticed. I felt like I was the only person going on about joy and that this simple powerful word was completely absent from our understanding of how children thrive. The truth is I was wrong. It turns out there are a lot of people talking about joy. There is an overwhelming concordance of evidence that tells us unambiguously and categorically that joyful experiences profoundly impact on children's learning, development and well-being. There are concrete links between positive experiences and life-long well-being, mental health and even physical health. There are numerous studies showing exactly how children learn and it is never, ever when they feel humiliated, bored, or unhappy.

The legend that is Greg Bottrill frequently talks about joy and creates joyful imaginative experiences for children. The awesome neuroscientist Judy Willis talks about the neuroscience of learning and backs it up with solid research based on copious studies showing unequivocally exactly how joy enhances every aspect of learning (Willis, 2007). The amazing Tamsin Grimmer, who is someone I feel genuinely privileged to have met, has actually published a book highlighting love as a pedagogy for working with children (Grimmer, 2021). It is well worth reading!

Other countries also seem to value joy. Joy is seen as an underpinning foundation for education in many Swedish schools for instance. In fact, almost every practitioner, trainer, keynote speaker and author I meet makes sure they implement joyful experiences for their children.

So, no more excuses. Let's go for it. Let's use joy as a guiding principle for all of our interactions with children because it will change children's lives. Every seemingly unanswered question about improving outcomes for children can be emphatically answered. With joy! How do we engage children in maths? With joyful experiences of maths. How do we get children outdoors more? With joyful outdoor experiences. How do we improve children's communication and language, physical activity levels, social skills, mental health, emotional well-being, learning, memory retention, creativity, problem solving, imagination, cultural capital, aspirations, behaviour and overall experience of childhood? With JOY! This is not a made-up concept, not an abstract idea, but a definable and essential process and fundamental foundation for every aspect of well-being and development.

Using the simple ideas outlined in this book I am more determined than ever to make sure that every child I work with, regardless of their vulnerability, experiences joy. My remit has always been to give children back their childhood, but I now know that what I have been doing for 32 years is giving children joy.

I caterpillar!

On one of our sessions supporting disabled children a young girl with profound and multiple learning disabilities climbed into one of the pop-up tunnels we had brought as part of our kit. We initially thought she was hiding because the noise and bustle of the session had become too much for her. A muffled voice then came from the tunnel saying, 'I a caterpillar and I hungry!' We then spent over thirty minutes feeding her on teddies until she climbed out of the tunnel and announced, 'I a butterfly now!' Her parents were utterly astounded. They had never seen her so engaged in play before, using such advanced imagination and communication skills. This is what joy does for our children if adults support it.

The best thing is that it is really simple. The three aspects of joy are essential to our children's experiences and easy to implement with a little imagination and a lot of patience. Feeling happiness and contentment, whilst being stimulated and engaged with an underlying ethos of emotional safety, are simple tools we can all easily apply to our everyday interactions with children.

And always remember another simple equation. If a child has more positive experiences of life than negative, then they are more likely to thrive. If, however, they have more negative than positive, they are more likely to struggle. One of our core remits should therefore be to make sure a child has as many positive experiences as possible to outweigh the negative.

In addition to the aspects of joy, several key themes have been discussed throughout this book and these make up a loose set of principles of joy.

The principles of joy

1. See the world through the eyes of a child and support and validate children's joy by sharing it with them. Do not undermine joy simply because we are adults.
2. Children are human beings with rights and needs and we should never treat them as anything other than that. If we wouldn't behave in a certain way to an adult, then we should not be doing it with children.
3. Constantly ask the question, *'How would I feel if?'* If a practice or experience would make you feel amazing then go for it. If a practice would make you feel anxious or excluded, then do not continue the practice with children.
4. Prioritise children. Make sure experiences are for children not for the benefit of the adults. Not allowing a child to play with sand because it makes a mess is prioritising the very adult concept of 'tidiness' rather than the joy of playing with sand. Joy can be messy.

5. Make time for joy. In a busy stressful day, we need to make sure there are moments of joy for our children every single day. Every aspect of planning, from choice of resources to activities and experiences should make sure there is sufficient joy. Remember surprising happiness is more powerful than the ordinary happiness.

6. Never ever withhold joyful experiences as a punishment or deterrent. Joyful experiences should be for all children, not just well-behaved ones.

7. Help children to see the beauty in the world especially if their childhood experiences have shown them the opposite. Awe and wonder is profoundly important.

8. If a learning opportunity does not involve joy, it will not be as effective. Rethink and try again.

9. Change the environment, both human and physical, to suit the child; do not try to change the child to fit the environment.

10. Don't be afraid to experiment and try new ways to engage your children. If you hold to the principles of joy, then it will not harm the children if something doesn't work but it will inspire them when it does.

11. Sing more, dance more and laugh more. Create an environment of laughter and children will thrive.

12. Stand up for joy and fight for joy. Challenge adults who take the joy away from children and bring them to task. Children rarely have the power to stand up to adults, so we need to do it for them. Every single child deserves, needs and has a fundamental right to a joyful childhood.

So, despite the fact that there are actually a lot of people going on about joy, it is still not recognised by the EYFS or the curriculum. I have a cunning plan though. Most early years settings will have the Characteristics of Effective Learning document displayed somewhere in the setting. It may be in plain view on a staff notice board or even on the back of the toilet door. It may be in a locked filing cabinet with a sign on the door saying, 'Beware of the leopard'. (A subtle *Hitch Hikers Guide to the Galaxy* reference – a source of shared joy between my late father and me.) Wherever that document is, you need to sneak into the setting in the dead of night, and graffiti the word 'joy' at the bottom. Because we now know, joy is the fourth characteristic of effective learning!

Now I don't want anyone to get into trouble, so make sure you wear a disguise – a fake beard and eye patch as a bare minimum. If you don't have the Characteristics of Effective Learning in your setting then find any official looking document and add the word 'joy'. The amazing author and childcare consultant Dr Sue Allingham has already written this on her Ofsted inspection handbook! But don't stop there. Put it on your staff notice board, your parent notice board, and your welcome sign. Add it to your menu and your planning sheets, your walls, doors and furniture. In fact, why not go out and get a tattoo done? On your forehead?

The Characteristics of Effective Learning

Playing and exploring
- Finding out and exploring
- Playing with what they know
- Being willing to have a go

Active learning
- Being involved and concentrating
- Keeping trying
- Enjoying achieving what they set out to do

Creating and thinking critically
- Having their own ideas
- Making links
- Choosing to do things

Figure 9.1 The Characteristics of Effective Learning – JOY!

What have you done today…

I recently went to see my daughter performing at a Young Voices event at a huge arena in Birmingham. I did not know what to expect and if I am being honest, I was not looking forward to the event as I usually find these kinds of things dull. Now don't get me wrong, I enjoy watching my own children perform (a bit) but sitting through other people's children can be really boring. I have just realised this makes me sound like a very bad person for which I can only apologise. It was not at all what I expected. If you have never sat in a venue the size of a small village whilst 6,000 children sing together in absolute joy then I cannot accurately describe to you just how moving and incredible this was, but I will try. Imagine a wall of joy hitting your ears like a throbbing hug from a dragon, moving through your body like a rumbling giant centipede (with googly eyes) and then echoing around the arena like the after-tremors from an exploding supernova. Something like that anyway.

One of the many high points was the actual Heather Small singing 'Proud' with 6,000 children as her backing singers. It was a moment of true magic and pure joy.

So, let's imagine a world where not just 6,000 children but all children experience joy every single day. Let's reimagine childhood so that even our most vulnerable children experience joy. The tenner in the pocket feeling, the first pop of the bubble feeling. What would this world look like? I believe that a world where all of our children experience joy is a world where children thrive, succeed and pass that joy on to the next generation, and the next. I believe if we all make that choice to support joy then the whole world can be and will be a better place to live.

So? What are you waiting for? Go out and spread some joy!

APPENDIX

Jazz Hands Dinosaur

In the deepest darkest forest a long time ago,
Lives a very special dinosaur who loves dancing to-and-fro,
He never wears a frown and is never heard to roar,
Because he's the one and only jazz hands dinosaur!

Who's that shimmying across the lands?
It's jazz hands dinosaur!
Who's that grooving and waving his hands?
It's jazz hands dinosaur!

He's got sequins on his arms and glitter on his toes,
A big feather boa and a ring through his nose,
He wears a fetching hat and a ruby on each claw,
Because he's the one and only jazz hands dinosaur!

Who's that shimmying across the lands?
It's jazz hands dinosaur!
Who's that grooving and waving his hands?
It's jazz hands dinosaur!

Whilst the other dinos stomp about following the crowd,
Jazzy dances freely and always sings out loud,
He flashes a toothy grin as he twirls across the floor,
Because he's the one and only jazz hands dinosaur!

Who's that shimmying across the lands?
It's jazz hands dinosaur!
Who's that grooving and waving his hands?
It's jazz hands dinosaur!

So if you think that dinosaurs are serious and dull,
Remember that there's one who always lives life to the full,
Dancing and jiving you'll never hear him snore,
Because he's the one and only jazz hands dinosaur!

Who's that shimmying across the lands?
It's jazz hands dinosaur!
Who's that grooving and waving his hands?
It's jazz hands dinosaur!

Written by Ben Kingston-Hughes

Song can be downloaded for free from our website www.inspiredchildren.org.
uk (click on 'Resources').

REFERENCES

American Physiological Society (2008, 10 April). Anticipating a laugh reduces our stress hormones, study shows. *ScienceDaily*. www.sciencedaily.com/releases/2008/04/080407114617.htm

BBC Four (2022, 23 February). Mission: Joy – with Archbishop Desmond Tutu and the Dalai Lama [Video]. www.bbc.co.uk/iplayer/episode/m0014rhk/mission-joy-with-archbishop-desmond-tutu-and-the-dalai-lama

Berk, L. S., Tan, S. A., Fry, W. F., Napier, B. J., Lee, J. W., Hubbard, R. W., Lewis, J. E., & Eby, W. C. (1989). Neuroendocrine and stress hormone changes during mirthful laughter. *The American Journal of the Medical Sciences*, 298(6), 390–396. https://doi.org/10.1097/00000441-198912000-00006

British Heart Foundation National Centre for Physical Activity and Health (2015). Physical activity in the early years, National Centre for Sport and Exercise Medicine (NCSEM). https://ncsem-em.org.uk/wp-content/uploads/2020/11/early-years-evidence-briefing.pdf

Colino, S. (2022, 26 April). How stress can damage your brain and body. *Washington Post*. www.washingtonpost.com/wellness/2022/04/26/inner-workings-stress-how-it-affects-your-brain-body/

Daywalt, D. and Jeffers, O. (2015). *The Day the Crayons Quit*. Glasgow: Harper Collins.

Daywalt, D. and Jeffers, O. (2015). *The Day the Crayons Came Home*. London: Philomel Books.

Department of Health and Social Care (2020). Physical activity guidelines: UK chief medical officers' report. www.gov.uk/government/publications/physical-activity-guidelines-uk-chief-medical-officers-report

Duffy, B. (2004) *All About Messy Play*. Nursery World, 4th November, pp. 15–22.

Duffy, B. (2007). All about... messy play. https://www.nurseryworld.co.uk/news/article/a-fine-mess-1

Dunbar, R. I. M., Baron, R., Frangou, A., Pearce, E., van Leeuwen, E. J. C., Stow, J., Partridge, G., MacDonald, I., Barra, V., & van Vugt, M. (2011). Social laughter is correlated with an elevated pain threshold, *Proceedings of the Royal Society B: Biological Sciences*, 279(1731), 1161–1167. https://doi.org/10.1098/rspb.2011.1373

Dunn, O. (nd). Learning English through sharing rhymes. *LearnEnglish Kids*. https://learnenglishkids.britishcouncil.org/parents/helping-your-child/learning-english-through-sharing-rhymes

Dweck, C. (2012). *Mindset: How You Can Fulfil Your Potential*. London: Robinson.

Early Years Alliance (2018, 3 June) Minds matter: The impact of working in the early years sector on practitioners' mental health and wellbeing. childcare-canada.*org, a project of the Childcare Resource and Research Unit*. https://childcarecanada.org/documents/research-policy-practice/18/06/minds-matter-impact-working-early-years-sector

Edwards, A. J., & Lieberman, J. N. (2014). *Playfulness: Its Relationship to Imagination and Creativity*. Elsevier Science & Technology Books.

Fryer, J. (2021), Was Edward de Bono, who has died at 88, a genius or just a master of gibberish? *Daily Mail Online*. www.dailymail.co.uk/news/article-9694895/Was-Edward-Bono-died-88-genius-just-master-gibberish.html

George Scarlett, W., Naudeau, S., Salonius-Pasternak, D., & Ponte, I. (Eds.) (2005). *Children's Play*. Thousand Oaks, CA: Sage Publications.

Grimmer, T. (2021). *Developing a Loving Pedagogy in the Early Years: How Love Fits with Professional Practice*. Taylor & Francis Group.

Grosz, S. (2013). *Examined Life: How We Lose and Find Ourselves*. W.W. Norton & Company, Incorporated.

Habibi, A., Cahn, B. R., Damasio, A., & Damasio, H. (2016). Neural correlates of accelerated auditory processing in children engaged in music training, *Developmental Cognitive Neuroscience, 21*, 1-14. doi:10.1016/j.dcn.2016.04.003

Hadaway, P. F., Alexander, B. K., Coambs, R. B., & Beyerstein, B. (1979). The effect of housing and gender on preference for morphine-sucrose solutions in rats. *Psychopharmacology, 66*(1), 87-91. doi:10.1007/BF00431995

Hughes, B. (2002). *A Playworker's Taxonomy of Play Types*, 2nd edition, London: PlayLink.

Kingston-Hughes, B. (2021). *A Very Unusual Journey into Play*. Thousand Oaks, CA: Corwin.

Krulwich, R. (2014). The list of animals who can truly, really dance is very short. Who's on it?, *NPR*. www.npr.org/sections/krulwich/2014/04/01/297686709/the-list-of-animals-who-can-truly-really-dance-is-very-short-who-s-on-it

Manninen, S., Tuominen, L., Dunbar, R. I., Karjalainen, T., Hirvonen, J., Arponen, E., Hari, R., Jääskeläinen, I. P., Sams, M., & Nummenmaa, L. (2017). Social laughter triggers endogenous opioid release in humans. *The Journal of Neuroscience, 37*(25), 6125-6131. https://doi.org/10.1523/jneurosci.0688-16.2017

Nicholson, S. (1971) How Not to Cheat Children. The Theory of Loose Parts Play. *Landscape Architecture, 62*, 30-34.

Office for Health Improvement Disparities (nd). Physical activity data tool: Statistical commentary, January 2022. www.gov.uk/government/statistics/physical-activity-data-tool-january-2022-update/physical-activity-data-tool-statistical-commentary-january-2022

Panksepp, J. and Biven, L. (2012) *The Archaeology of Mind: Neuroevolutionary Origins of Human Emotion*. London: W.W. Norton & Co.

Phoenix, S. (2021). From behaviour 'management' to fostering wellbeing: A way forward. *Educating Young Children*, 27(2), 20-23.

Popova, M. (2013, 23 May). Presence, not praise: How to cultivate a healthy relationship with achievement. *The Marginalian*. www.themarginalian. org/2013/05/23/stephen-grosz-examined-life/

Robinson, L. (2018, 2 November). Laughter is the best medicine. HelpGuide.*org*. www.helpguide.org/articles/mental-health/laughter-is-the-best-medicine. htm

Vygotsky, L. S. (1978). *Mind in Society: The Development of Higher Psychological Processes*. Cambridge, MA: Harvard University Press.

Willis, J. (2007, 1 June). The neuroscience of joyful education. *ASCD*. www.ascd. org/el/articles/the-neuroscience-of-joyful-education

INDEX